TIME TO HEAL

Better me, better world,
through the astonishing new
science of self-healing

Dr Robin Youngson

Rebelheart Publishers

Copyright © 2020 Robin Youngson

Edition 1-3
The moral rights of the author have been asserted

Published in New Zealand by:

Rebelheart Publishers
6 Norrie Avenue, Raglan 3225, New Zealand

Email: info@neuroscienceofhealing.com
Phone: 00 64 21 660 344

E-book edition available for purchase and download from neuroscienceofhealing.com

All rights reserved. No part of this book may be reproduced by any mechanical, photographic or electronic process or recording; nor may it be transmitted or otherwise be copied except for 'fair use' as brief quotations embodied in articles and reviews. The purchaser may store a pdf version of this book for private use only. Any exception requires prior written permission of the publisher.

Dr Robin Youngson is a Certified Practitioner of Havening Techniques®. Havening Techniques is a registered trade mark of Ronald Ruden, 15 East 91st Street, New York.
www.havening.org

Cover image: Alicia Khoo Photography

CONTENTS

Title Page
Copyright
Preface - please read
1. Choosing a better life	1
2. Struggling in life? It's not your fault!	6
3. Why trauma sabotages your happiness	23
4. The science behind this practice	51
5. The community impact of trauma	66
6. Making a personal commitment	73
7. My philosophy of practice	81
8. A better world starts with me	89
9. Finding help	104
More resources	110
Did you love my book?	112
About The Author	113
Praise For Author	117
Books By This Author	121

PREFACE - PLEASE READ

From my early days as a medical student, I felt deep empathy for the suffering of patients in the many hospitals and clinics where I trained. It was compassion that drew me into medicine, which is *'the human quality of understanding suffering and wanting to do something about it'*. Driven by that imperative, I have dedicated my whole career to improving the healthcare system, as well as caring for individual patients.

The meaning of healing is to transcend suffering. So the ultimate purpose of compassion is healing. My wife Meredith and I have travelled the world in our work to bring more humanity and compassion to healthcare. We have hosted workshops for thousands of health professionals in many countries, exploring stories of deep connection, compassion and healing. Those stories inspired in us a profound belief in the human power of healing, far beyond that recognized in mainstream medicine.

Many health professional are burning out because their workplaces have become harsh places where the focus is on technology and efficiency, not caring for human beings. Indeed to use the word '*healing*' is to be denigrated within the medical culture.

A few years ago, I was invited by the editors of a prestigious international medical journal to write an essay about the role of compassion in healthcare. I was elated because the medical profession had until this point ignored my work. I naively assumed that my paper would automatically be published, because it was commissioned by the editors; however, my manuscript went to peer reviewers who strongly criticized my essay.

One said, '*You should not use the word healing, because it has negative connotations*'. Also, he said that I was making many claims '*not backed up by evidence*'.

Another wrote '*You haven't mention the harmful side-effects of compassion and how dangerous it would be to show compassion to someone with a mental illness.*' My article was rejected and I felt angry and betrayed. It seemed to me that the very essence of my medical practice was being denied.

It's not as if I was a 'fringe' doctor. By training, I am an anesthesiologist with professional Fellowships in two countries. I began my specialist career in the biggest teaching hospital in New Zealand, providing anesthesia and intensive care for complex surgery and advanced trauma care. Also, I was the Clinical Leader for innovation and quality improvement as a member of the Hospital Executive Team.

I have also been an advisor to the New Zealand government, and the World Health Organization, on quality improvement and patient safety. I was the medical leader of a team that designed, built, commissioned and ran an entirely new hospital service for an underprivileged community.

I have thought deeply about the purpose of our work in healthcare and how best to support health and wellbeing in patient, families and communities. My new work represents the culmination of three decades of my exploration and learning.

What I share in this book, about the remarkable new science of self-healing, is pushing past the boundaries of what most doctors would believe. Sadly, the subject of self-healing is entirely missing from the curriculum of medical training. Mindful of the potential to miss my target, I sent the draft of my book to a diverse range of colleagues for review and feedback, asking people to be really honest.

The responses were deeply encouraging and, at the same time, alerted me to changes that could strengthen my book.

One reviewer said, '*You have made a lot of unsubstantiated assertions and I would have liked to see the evidence, up front, like your last book.*' This colleague has followed my work for many years, and I respect her opinion. She also said that my book would be more credible if I shared something of my life's work at the beginning of the book. So, I have taken up her suggestion, in adding this preface to my book.

I agree with my colleague that I am making claims that my medical peers would say are not yet 'evidence-based'. Today I'm thrilled to report publication of the first major scientific trial of the self-healing practice I describe in this book, showing remarkable results. None-the-less I am putting my reputation on the line and risk being dismissed by my medical peers.

This is not a new experience for me. I have spent many years speaking out on topics that my fellow doctors felt were non-scientific, woo-woo, irrelevant, or even threatening to the status quo. I had the audacity to suggest that healthcare as a whole, and the profession of medicine in particular, had lost its humanity and compassion.

Despite campaigning all around the world and speaking at hundreds of conferences on the topic of compassion and caring, my work was shunned by the medical profession for many years. Technical knowledge and skills, clinical detachment and objectivity were deemed to be the hallmarks of a good doctor, more than compassion and caring. Indeed many doctors believed that showing emotion or offering compassion was a sign of weakness.

Over time, I found ways to make my message more engaging and credible for my medical colleagues. I had to change myself to change the world. The story of my struggles, and eventual success, is told in my TEDx talk (https://youtu.be/jTYSzLtbYTU). In 2016, I was given the highest award by the New Zealand Medical Association for my work on compassion. I am now gladdened to hear my medical peers emphasizing care and compassion, when they speak at scientific and medical conferences.

Through the years, the way I relate to patients has changed profoundly. The heroic super-doctor, master of high-tech medicine, became much more gentle, compassionate and humane. From research and my own practice, I learned that my healing presence could have a dramatic impact not only on the experience of my patients, but on their clinical outcomes.

Compassionate caring reduces anxiety and pain, lessens the need for painkillers, prevents complications, promotes wound healing, hastens recovery, shortens hospital stays, and can even prolong life. I was becoming the healer I always wanted to be. I shared this new-found knowledge in my previous book, **TIME TO CARE – How to love your patients and your job**.'

The last two years have been a revelation for me. I am astounded to learn that the brain has a mechanism to rapidly heal emotional trauma. People can now potentially be cured of major anxiety, depression, PTSD, chronic pain, and a host of chronic physical illnesses that have their roots in prolonged stress and unhappiness. I see life-changing results in my clinic every day.

Therefore, I have quit my job as an anesthesiologist, to work full-time in this new healing practice, to care for clients, train others in the techniques, and hopefully to do clinical research trials.

This new book is the culmination of decades of my scientific learning and changing personal beliefs. In a way, everything I have done before has prepared me for this new adventure. I can't wait to share it with you.

Dr Robin Youngson
September 2020

1. CHOOSING A BETTER LIFE

When life is just an ongoing struggle, you can feel trapped with no space to make choices. Being stuck in chronic negative emotions such as anxiety, depression, hurt, or anger means that you are in the grip of emotional brain programming from the past that takes away your power.

Worse still, when you are anxious and stressed, your sensory systems switch into a survival mode where the sole focus of your nervous system is potential risk. Your brain no longer perceives opportunities and doesn't notice the good things in life.

The chronic stress takes a toll on your physical health. You feel exhausted, you don't sleep well, your body aches. Your digestion plays up, you get sick more often, and you become prone to addictions which add to the toll on your health.

I can explain how to get out of this trap. Your negative emotions are largely the result of your past emotional trauma. This book shares an amazing new scientific discovery: that all of us have a mechanism in the brain that can rapidly delete traumatic events from your memory, thus freeing you from the past.

This breakthrough is the work of a brilliant physician and PhD researcher in the USA, Dr Ronald Ruden. In Chapter Four, I explain all the science behind his inspiring work. The impact of his discoveries is life-changing. There are now hundreds of certified practitioners around the world offering the Havening Techniques® that Dr Ruden developed. As a Certified Havening Trainer, I'm thrilled to share this knowledge.

In my clinic I meet some clients who are so haunted by one traumatic event – such as a violent attack or rape – that they never feel safe. Yet fifteen minutes of guided self-healing can literally erase the trauma from their brain so they are freed from their past. It's as if the terrible event never happened. The fear is gone.

I have seen clients cured of severe anxiety disorders and PTSD. Depression can be banished when the underlying trauma is identified and healed. Broken relationships are healed when the inbuilt fears of abandonment or betrayal are erased.

Sometimes chronic pain and physical illness is the direct consequence of emotional trauma. Heal the trauma and the pain and illness vanish.

When your trauma is healed, you no longer experience the emotional reactions and stress responses that trap you in life struggles. The many situations and people that used to trigger your anxiety, anger or hurt no longer have any power over you. You can step forward calmly and confidently.

Suddenly you have power to make choices again. Imagine how liberating that would be!

Life possibilities open up. You see things more clearly. You perceive many opportunities that were hidden before. You gain the power to make plans and decisions. You realize how much of the world you saw was created by your own attitudes and beliefs. Now the world looks very different.

Do you really want your power back? Are you ready to be responsible for your life? This is the first choice that you have to make. It's a major life decision. If you are ready, it's my privilege to be your guide.

This book is for those who say, '*I choose a better me!*'

Why I love this work so much

Many of my clients really struggle in life, and not through lack of trying to get their lives back on track. I see clients like you who invest in their health, who eat good food, exercise regularly, go to yoga classes, they have good friends – but somehow their struggles go on. Many have sought counseling or therapy, often without much relief.

It's hard to convey how much gratitude I feel when I see people finding hope again: it's a privilege to show how this new science explains your life difficulties, to let you know it's not your fault, to describe how your brain can rapidly heal trauma, and then to demonstrate your self-healing capacity.

Many of my clients are astonished by the end of their first session in my clinic. A memory that haunted them is simply erased. An overwhelming burden of negative emotions is lifted. Their phobia is cured.

Of course, some clients have layers of trauma, starting early in life. So we can begin a patient and gentle process to heal that trauma, layer by layer, over a number of sessions. My clients see the changes happening in their lives; they notice their anxiety reducing, their hurt easing, their anger abating.

For clients in life crisis, I offer one-on-one healing retreats. In one week, you can completely change the trajectory of your life. What would that be worth? Don't you owe it to yourself?

As I explore in the next chapter, '*It's not your fault*', very many of your life difficulties are the result of emotional programming in your brain. You are literally hard-wired to react in certain ways. The hard-wiring doesn't just affect your emotions, it also controls many of your body reactions, motivations and behaviours.

Science can now tell us exactly how this programming works in the brain – and why – and how we can heal ourselves to erase these unhelpful 'programs' that drive our life. This is the understanding that underpins my healing practice.

I see my clients leaving their past behind and floating free to shine as the very best version of themselves. They are liberated and energized to offer their gifts, and to find renewed meaning and purpose in life.

The ripple effects are enormous. They literally transform the relationships around them. They bring out the best in others, create loving relationships, and inspire others to change.

So this decision is not just for you. It's also making a commitment to create a more beautiful world around you. This may be the greatest gift you ever give your loved ones.

Are you ready to fulfill your life purpose? Do you want to be free? It's time to heal.

2. STRUGGLING IN LIFE? IT'S NOT YOUR FAULT!

What if your life struggles are not your fault? What if your life difficulties are programmed into your brain and are completely predictable? What if you could rapidly erase the harmful brain programs to unleash the very best version of yourself?

Your brain is already designed to do this.

It's my pleasure to show you how.

I have seen so many lives transformed. This is the most gratifying work I have done in more than thirty years as a doctor and international health leader.

I meet so many people struggling in life, just like you. What do I mean by life struggles? From the stories my clients tell me again and again, your life problems might feel like this:

- Your relationship has broken up and you feel lonely and worthless. It's happened again and again. You wonder, why do I keep choosing partners who treat me badly?
- Your love life is faltering because you are full of fears that your partner doesn't really love you, or is getting ready to dump you.
- You are overwhelmed with anxiety, stress, and negative emotions and you can't think your way out of it. Your job is becoming a nightmare.
- You feel lonely and alone and you'd love to make friends. But you feel so shy and awkward in social gatherings - you think, '*Nobody likes me.*'
- Your life was going OK and then one bad thing happened and suddenly you have fallen apart.
- You feel lost and confused, and lack a focus in life. You hesitate to start new things because a voice inside says, '*I'm not good enough.*' You feel depressed.
- It feels like the whole world is your responsibility so you try to do everything yourself. But who looks after you?
- You strive so hard to succeed and to prove

your worth that you're heading for exhaustion and burnout. Why do your accomplishments feel hollow?
- Your boss is a bully but you get the blame for being too sensitive. Loud and aggressive people make you feel anxious.
- You find yourself trapped in endless cycles of conflict and resentment with family members who are supposed to love you.
- You're full of negative self-talk and blame. You feel stupid, useless, worthless.
- You feel, deep down, that you don't deserve to be loved or to be happy. Your sense of self-worth is at an all-time low.

What if every one of these life problems can easily be explained? What if, through no fault of your own, your brain got programmed early in life to shape your emotional reactions and motivations to create every one of these situations?

You can't change these programs through *willpower* and you can't *rationalise* your way out of your problems. But you CAN rapidly erase these programs and set yourself free. This self-healing mechanism already exists in your brain.

These programmed emotional reactions chain you to the past, stuck in emotional responses from a time early in life when you felt vulnerable and insecure. What would it be like to sever the chains that hold you down and to float free as your true self?

This is what I see happening to my clients, and I can't tell you how amazing and joyful it is to witness that transformation. And they do all the healing themselves!

It feels like magic yet we know precisely how this works in the brain – right down to the level of molecular reactions – and we know how to activate and support this natural healing process.

Human beings are designed to heal!

- What if your self-doubt could be replaced with confidence?
- What if you could inspire loving and secure relationships?
- What if your stress and overwhelm could be replaced with energising engagement, a joyful life, and meaningful accomplishments?
- What if you could feel truly worthy, deserving of love, ready to fulfil your deepest purpose?

I'm so happy to share how this can work.

Why you can't rationalise your way out of your problems

How many self-help book do you have on your shelf? They are full of advice: *set goals, break down problems into little steps, reframe your thinking, write gratitude journals, do yoga, meditate, etc.* You probably tried all that already. These are useful tools but they don't solve the fundamental problem.

Most people assume that we should just *'think our way out of our problems.'* But positive self-talk without changing the inbuilt programming is little more use than the advice offered by our friends.

How many times have people said, *'You should just be more confident'*? Makes you feel worse, doesn't it. You can't magically be more confident any more that you can suddenly be taller. Your confidence, or lack of it, is hard-wired into your operating system and no amount of self-talk can change that. But what if you could quickly erase the program that saps your confidence?

How many times have people told you to chill out, when you are already in overwhelm: *'You should calm down!'* That doesn't help either. You don't choose your stress. After all, it's horrible to feel stressed.

The truth is, your anxiety and negative feelings are also programmed into your brain. No matter how hard you try, you can't talk your way out of your feelings in the moment.

I explain it to my clients like this: imagine you have a Microsoft Windows 10 computer, which has an operating system that determines exactly how the computer works. You download software programs to add functions and do useful stuff. But no matter how many software programs you download, it doesn't change the operating system of your computer: it's still Windows 10.

In your own brain, your conscious thoughts are like software and so they have little short-term influence on your brain's operating system. In contrast, emotional trauma is programmed into your brain at the level of the operating system. These are built-in, automatic functions. That's why talk therapy sometimes doesn't help much.

But what if you could simply delete the brain circuits in your operating system that program your anxiety and stress? That's what this healing practice does.

For the sake of argument, I have somewhat simplified matters here. Over the long term, is it possible to shape your emotional reactions through the focussed application of conscious thought processes. Thus a deliberate and sustained focus on kindness and gratitude can begin to reduce your negative feelings. But it's a lot easier and quicker to simply delete the cause of the negative emotions.

How do the negative programs in your brain actually work?

A part of our brain called the **amygdala** serves as our safety warning system, ever-alert to potential threats in life, ready to react within seconds. This primitive part of the brain has evolved to protect us from predators and other risks to our survival. It alerts us to dangers so we can take action before it's too late.

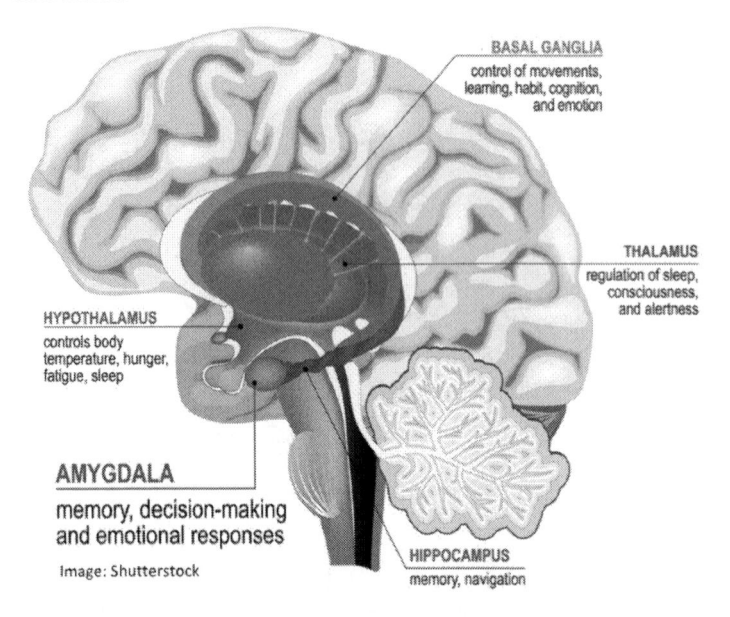

BASAL GANGLIA
control of movements, learning, habit, cognition, and emotion

THALAMUS
regulation of sleep, consciousness, and alertness

HYPOTHALAMUS
controls body temperature, hunger, fatigue, sleep

AMYGDALA
memory, decision-making and emotional responses

Image: Shutterstock

HIPPOCAMPUS
memory, navigation

This system *learns* about potential threats, through experience. So if a young animal is chased by a predator and manages to get away, the amygdala will store every detail of the near-miss event to trigger instant warnings in the future. It might be the smell of the predator, or a certain location, or time of day that serves as warnings.

Because our survival is at risk, this system can instantly highjack our emotions and our body systems to respond to threat.

2. STRUGGLING IN LIFE? IT'S NOT YOU...

It's not only physical threats that get stored. Because we are social animals and we depend on others for survival, we are powerfully triggered by threats to our relationships. So we are deeply fearful of abandonment, or betrayal, or threats of violence. The amygdala is the place where we store emotional trauma and activate the programmed emotional reactions. A good example is the traumatic impact of childhood bullying.

Feelings like anxiety, fear or alarm mean that we are instantly motivated to focus on a potential or actual threat. Our body is readied for action – the so-called '*fight or flight*' response.

A cascade of nerve signals and stress hormones shapes our body response: blood flow is increased in muscles, our heart and breathing speed up, we mobilise energy stores, and shut down non-immediate survival functions such as digestion.

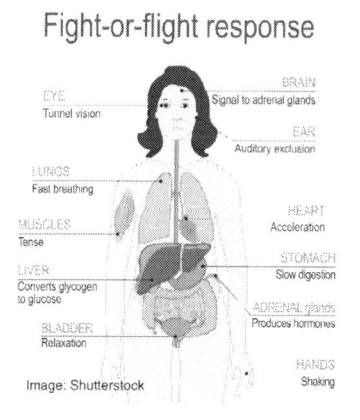

Fight-or-flight response

EYE
Tunnel vision

BRAIN
Signal to adrenal glands

EAR
Auditory exclusion

LUNGS
Fast breathing

MUSCLES
Tense

HEART
Acceleration

LIVER
Converts glycogen to glucose

STOMACH
Slow digestion

ADRENAL glands
Produces hormones

BLADDER
Relaxation

HANDS
Shaking

Image: Shutterstock

Our eyesight, hearing and other senses cone down

to focus only on the threat, and we ignore other sensory information coming in. When our offspring or loved ones are threatened, we may erupt in defensive rage.

The freeze response

When threat is completely overwhelming, we lose the capacity to fight or to flee. Our body goes into the most severe form of emotional shock, where we become temporarily immobilised and frozen. In the most extreme version we collapse, our heart beat and breathing almost stop, and most of our brain functions goes off-line. We may dissociate and have an out of body experience.

Thus when people with severe trauma and PTSD are triggered, they may experience completely opposite reactions. Some will activate the flight-and-flight system and erupt in fear and rage. Others will freeze and dissociate, a state of profound vulnerability and helplessness.

All these reactions are completely automatic, they are hard-wired responses in our brain's operating system. One of the ways we can know we are reacting in this way is that we always feel it in our body.

Innate fears and learned fears

We are born with this alarm system already operational. New babies have certain kinds of threats already programmed, which are called '*innate*' or '*unconditional*' threats. Thus babies are automatically afraid of things that cause physical pain, of suffocation, of abandonment, of falling from a height, and of certain kinds of predators.

Other threats stored in our alarm system are *learned* threats; we acquire these fears as a result of life experiences. So, for instance, if you point a gun at a baby there is no fear reaction. But if you point a gun at an adult, the fear is immediate because we have learned that a gun can instantly injure or kill us. So a gun becomes a learned threat.

The process of learning and storing new threats in our amygdala alarm system is completely automatic. We all intuitively know that a traumatic event can be stored almost instantly in our brain, to haunt us for a lifetime. That's because, when we experience strong negative emotions such as fear, we create what is known as a '*traumatic memory*' which is stored differently from ordinary memories.

In fact, our brain remembers much more than we know. During traumatic events our brain creates a kind of multi-media image of the event, which binds together all the elements – the sights, sounds, smells, and body sensations - which make up our sensory information about the trauma, and all of our internal responses such as emotions, feelings and stress reactions.

Every detail of the external environment, the context and setting of the trauma, is stored as part of the alarm system. This information becomes the basis for subconscious triggers that can activate our alarm circuits.

Here's a simple example. A client came to me with a lot of anxiety and tension, connected with driving or being a passenger in a car. It started ten years before, when she was an innocent victim of a car accident.

She was stationary at a road junction, waiting to turn, when an unseen speeding driver suddenly smashed into her car, spinning her violently around. She wasn't injured, other than some mild whiplash, but her car was written off.

She told me that she became very anxious when driving a car and that a long journey was a bad ordeal. She gets a fright if a car suddenly appears around a corner. At other times, when not in a car, she startles and gets a fear reaction from sudden noises or movement.

Her car accident caused a traumatic memory to be

encoded in her amygdala. This memory included all the details of the context, setting and event, together with her emotional and body reactions to the accident. Thus, she had an alarm circuit, hardwired in her brain, that caused an immediate fear reaction if any sensory information unconsciously reminded her of the accident.

Thus the smells, seated posture, engine noises, and sights of the car interior trigger her alarm circuits, making her feel anxious. A sudden movement, or unexpected noise, reminds her of the terrifying moment of collision, which triggers an immediate fear reaction.

Her brain has created a programmed reaction, caused by hard-wired nerve connections, which links certain kinds of sensory input (unconscious triggers) to the automatic reaction: powerful negative emotions, body reactions and stress responses. No wonder her car journeys were exhausting and nerve wracking! My client is a very smart and resourceful person and yet, no matter how hard she tried, she couldn't talk her way out of her fear and anxiety.

Happily, in just fifteen minutes of guided self-healing, we deleted the nerve connections that formed the alarm circuit in her amygdala. There is no longer a link between the sensory triggers and the fear response, and she can now drive a car without anxiety or fear.

Sometimes the trigger can be very subtle, a tone of voice, a certain body posture, a colour or a smell. Or it can be remarkably specific. In recent times, I was working in a public hospital as an anesthesiologist, involved in routine, low-risk day surgery. I'm very experienced so this is usually relaxing and easy work. However, I noticed that I had an unaccountable tension and feeling of stress arriving for work each day.

I was puzzled by my reaction until I used my knowledge of trauma to work out the trigger. In my hospital, I had to climb four flights of stairs before entering the changing room of the operating department. Casting my mind back more than thirty years, I recalled that during my very stressful first year as a doctor, I often felt very anxious going into the operating rooms. In that hospital, I also had to climb *four flights of stairs* to reach the changing room!

Thus my first year of medical training had created a traumatic memory that included the context – working in a hospital – the fear-inducing events in the operating room, and a closely connected activity – climbing the stairs – that became the subconscious trigger.

I sought the help of a colleague and in a few minutes

we erased the traumatic memory of my visits to the operating room as a junior doctor. The very next day I arrived at work in the operating room, relaxed and at ease, and the stress feelings never came back.

In the life difficulties you experience, subconscious triggers are likely causing automatic emotional and body reactions that create the problems you are experiencing.

Here are some examples of the kind of traumatic experiences and associated triggers, which link to the life problems I listed earlier:

- If you're the person who felt anxious, intimidated and bullied by your boss or a workmate, you very likely had experiences of being frightened by an adult when you were a child, such as a parent who came home drunk, loud and aggressive. The workplace trigger might be the loud voice, or the angry body posture, or the criticism.

- If you have fears of abandonment, maybe when you were small, your parents gave all their attention to your sick little sister - in and out of hospital - so you felt unseen and neglected. Or your parents split up when you were small; or one of your parents died when you were young. Your childhood emotional needs for love and security were not met at a formative time of your life. Now, as an adult, any small threat to your relationship can trigger an overwhelming fear.

- Perhaps you are one of the many people who never feels good enough? You hesitate to start a new project because you subconsciously feel it won't be good enough, or people won't like it. If your boss give you some helpful criticism about your latest work assignment, you feel crushed. In this case, it's possible that you had parents who gave you praise and approval for achievements but didn't validate your emotions and feelings.

- Maybe you are like one of my clients who was terribly anxious and fearful about his health. He'd get tight in the chest, he found it hard to breathe, his heart would pound, and he'd be convinced he was having a heart attack. In all the many visits to his doctor the tests came back normal but the reassuring words from his doctor really didn't help. He knew he was sick and dying, despite being a young man. Suppressed in his memory was a terrifying experience, as a seven-year-old boy, seeing his grandfather die in hospital, gasping for breath.

One of the patterns you might notice is that almost all of these reactions spring from childhood experiences. When I ask my clients how old they feel, when they are in the grip of negative emotions, they often tell me that they sense a small, child-like part of themselves.

Fortunately we all have a healing mechanism in our brain, which is specifically designed to rapidly erase traumatic memories and to delete the programs that hold us back.

Thus the client with a bullying boss has lost all her fear. She now has a powerful sense of her self-worth, and she can confidently assert herself. The tables are turned.

The client with a string of broken relationships and serial abandonments has now found true love with a man who loves and respects her. All her best qualities shine out of her. If they have a dispute, she can calmly resolve it, with empathy and understanding.

The client who never felt good enough has just finished writing her first book. She writes with humour, compassion and insight to create delightful characters to entertain her readers. Her creativity is in full flow.

And the client with all the scary health issues hasn't needed to see his doctor for more than a year. All the symptoms are gone. Indeed, when a friend got sick, he was the one who visited her in hospital and helped her recover.

You might be wondering if you are suffering from emotional triggers that link to past trauma? You can often pick up the clues yourself.

Often there is a pattern of behaviour, you find yourself having the same kind of emotional reactions again and again. That's because the triggers are usually very specific to a situation. Also, you usually feel the reaction in your body – there is a physical stress response accompanying the strong emotions.

An experienced practitioner will listen to your stories and pick up these patterns, even if you are not sure where they come from.

In all the examples I shared, my clients have lost their automatic reactions and now they are free to respond in an adult way. That's what responsible means, *'the ability to respond, rather than react.'*

Why are these miraculous transformations surprising? If you think about it, it makes NO sense that we didn't evolve a mechanism to heal our trauma, over millions of years of evolution! It's just that doctors are exclusively trained to diagnose and treat disease and illness, and never learn anything about the self-healing capacity of their patients.

In the next chapter I'll explain how emotional trauma can take away your power to make choices and sabotage your happiness. Later on in the book, we'll look at the science behind this self-healing mechanism in our brains.

3. WHY TRAUMA SABOTAGES YOUR HAPPINESS

We all want to be happy in life. If we look at the components of happiness, we can understand exactly why your programmed emotional reactions stop you being happy and successful. Before we get into that, here's an outline of the science of happiness.

About twenty years ago, the new field of positive psychology was launched. Until the late 1990's, almost all the research and therapy in psychology was focused on deficits and pathologies – all the ways human beings can be anxious, angry, sad or unhappy. Dr Martin Seligman is the founding father of a whole new way of looking at things called 'Positive Psychology'.

'*What do we need to flourish?*' he asked. How can we build resilience, wellbeing, happiness, joy, courage, compassion – and all the other human elements of psychological wellbeing?

Based on his decades of research, he came up with a scientific model for happiness and flourishing called **PERMA**:
- **P**ositive emotions
- **E**ngagement
- **R**elationships
- **M**eaning in life
- **A**ccomplishments.

You can read more about Seligman's model of happiness at PositivePsychology.com

Positive Emotions
When you are flourishing you have lots of positive emotions, not just being joyful and happy but also feeling optimistic and positive. Even in the event of difficult life challenges, you remain hopeful for the future. You see the best in every situation, not the worst. Rather than focusing on fears and risks, your perception widens to see many more potential benefits and opportunities.

Engagement
When you are feeling unhappy, it's often because you are ruminating on hurts from the past, or

worrying about the future. The antidote to this unhappy preoccupation is being fully engaged, in the present moment, in an activity that is absorbing and enjoyable. It's those times when you are completely engrossed in playing a sport or a musical instrument, absorbed in an interesting project, or giving full attention to another person. Time passes without you noticing, you forget about your worries, and you find yourself in a state of flow and creativity. That happy state is called engagement.

Relationships
Western culture has a focus on individuality and competition – striving to get ahead. We seek happiness in our possessions or status. But science shows that we are deeply social creatures who need meaningful relationships to thrive. We need intimacy and connection, and our true happiness comes from being kind, caring and compassionate towards others. This is deeply part of our biology and we even have hormones – such as oxytocin – that both activate and reward close bonding with others. When a new baby is born, the mother gets a huge surge of oxytocin, which creates that blissful state of love and bonding. Positive relationships give us true happiness.

Meaning
Meaning gives us direction in life; it helps you make life decisions and resolve conflicts. It answers the question: 'Why am I here? What is the purpose of

my life?' If you can find a foundation of meaning in life, then you will know how to use your gifts to fulfil your purpose. Meaning arises from a sense of deep connection, of belonging to something bigger than yourself. Some find meaning in religion or a spiritual practice, or through working for a good company or organisation, raising children, volunteering, or doing good in the world.

Accomplishments
Happiness is not only in the present moment. You gain satisfaction when you can look back on a life well lived, when you remember your accomplishments with satisfaction and pride, when you know that all your efforts and hard work made a positive difference. Happiness comes from reaching your full potential, when you have the sense of living as the best possible version of yourself.

These five pillars of happiness are all interdependent. When you have deep meaning in life, it's easy to be fully engaged in activities. Your relationships are more successful when you have positive emotions. When you can work well with others, you are more likely to have meaningful accomplishments. And so on.

But every one of these pillars of happiness is undermined when you have trauma encoded in your brain.

How your trauma stops you from being happy

It's a simple matter to understand how your encoded emotional trauma can sabotage every pillar of happiness. Let's look at the five pillars in turn:

1. How Positive Emotions are affected

Trauma always involves negative emotions, such as anxiety, fear, pain, abandonment, anger, betrayal, or other forms of hurt. So these are the emotions that get encoded in the amygdala and are easily activated by subconscious triggers in our everyday life. For some people, the stress activation is almost continuous, and they are anxious in every waking moment. Others have situational anxiety or stress, such as at work. Some people are consumed with anger.

Positive emotions don't get encoded as trauma, only the negative feelings. So those who have traumatic events in life, or an upbringing that didn't meet their emotional needs, tend to have lots of negative emotions. It's hard to feel happy if you are constantly filled with hurt, anger or anxiety.

Also, the more time we spend ruminating on what makes us unhappy, the more we grow new nerve connections in the part of the brain associated with negative feelings, while the part of the brain responsible for positive feelings actually starts to shrink. These changes are reversible, in just the same way we can regain physical fitness and build our muscles.

Imagine how much better life could be if the things that trigger your anxiety or anger simply don't have that power any more? You could be freed from your burden of negative emotions and free to choose how best to respond, rather than just react.

Image: Shutterstock

The latest neuroscience tells us exactly how to erase the programs that hold negative emotions.

> **By the way...**
> Positive emotions and positive triggers also get encoded in your brain, in a way that is the

complete opposite of trauma. As an adult, I feel instantly happy when I get on my bicycle, an association with childhood memories of carefree days exploring the neighbourhood on my bike.

When we have loving relationships, we encode these also, as a way of being. We start to replace some of our negative programming with positive programs.

2. Why it's so hard to get Engaged

I am struck by how many of my clients feel paralysed in their lives. They have talents to offer and worthwhile projects to get started, or activities they would find pleasurable, if only they were motivated to make a start. They have lost the power to make good choices.

Almost always, the procrastination is based on a fear of failure, or lack of approval, or fear of getting negative feedback or criticism. *What if my work isn't good enough? What if nobody likes it? What if my friends don't really want to spend time with me?* This is how lack of confidence works.

If you feel like this, you probably had an upbringing where you won approval for your accomplishments, rather than emotional validation. In your childhood mind, being loved depended on doing well and winning praise from your parents or teachers. Any criticism felt like rejection or being labelled stupid or worthless. So, as an adult, trying anything new that might be judged as 'not good enough', feels emotionally risky.

I remember my Dad trying to coach me in solving math problems when I was small. When I was reluctant to venture an answer that might be wrong, he only made the potential humiliation worse by telling me how easy the problem was! In a kindly way he was trying to encourage me but the effect was the opposite of what he intended. I would clam right up.

I was never confident enough to make mistakes, a characteristic that lasted well into my adult years. I became a perfectionist, which meant that I became hyper-critical of my efforts and wasted enormous amounts of time and energy without adding any real value to my task. How freeing it was to learn to be content with just doing 'good enough' - which probably is pretty good anyway!

When we let go of the self-criticism, and trying to achieve perfection, we often become more authentic. My most popular YouTube video on self-healing was created in an hour. I had no script, it was hastily set up, and the technical quality isn't great. But I decided to let go of my attempts to create the perfect video and upload it to YouTube anyway. I have been amazed by how much people love the video! My carefully scripted videos just don't elicit the same response.

In extreme cases of emotional trauma, people learn to dissociate, or even freeze. Any kind of meaningful engagement becomes impossible. Some people even feel that they don't deserve to be happy, or to partake in activities that give them pleasure. All these states completely inhibit engagement.

What if all these mental blocks could simply be erased? What if you could have the confidence to launch into new activities without worrying about how people might judge you? What if you could be joyfully engaged in life?

I have seen many clients step forward confidently. We know how to delete these blocks to engagement.

3. How your Relationships get sabotaged

The three worst poisons for healthy relationships that arise out of traumatic experiences are abuse, abandonment, and betrayal. We'll look at each in turn.

Physical and sexual abuse

According to RAINN (Rape, Abuse & Incest National Network) in the USA, 1-in-6 American women have been the victim of an attempted or completed rape. Of the women who seek help in my clinic, about 1 in 3 reveal a history of sexual abuse or violence.

> At this point, I want to make clear that the self healing practice I offer does NOT ever require you to tell the story of your abuse. I have met so many clients who have been re-traumatised by having to tell their shameful and humiliating stories to psychiatrists, therapists or counsellors.

Many other clients report physical abuse or neglect in their childhood. The impact is enormous. Victims of sexual or physical abuse report high rates of emotional distress, symptoms of PTSD, thoughts of suicide, illegal drug use, relationship difficulties at work and home, and a host of other life difficulties.

An example life story

Here's an example of the devastation caused by sexual violence. Mandy (not her real name) is a grade-A college student, flying through all her exams, top of the class, excelling in sports and physical activities, multi-talented and beautiful. She is also a lovely, caring and generous person. She has everything in life going for her. She comes from a family and cultural background that values hard work, high achievement and status. She is perhaps a little over-driven to succeed.

At college, she was raped after a party. This event was very shameful for her and she told nobody. Being very determined, she overcame her trauma and got on with life. But the traumatic imprint of this event remained in her mind. A few months later, she was the victim of a second sexual assault, physically less serious but emotionally devastating.

Her life fell apart. She failed all her exams and was dismissed from college. She began drinking heavily and taking drugs. She nearly died after a prescription drug overdose. She lost all hope and was spiralling into deep despair, reckless behaviour and probable suicide. She refused to talk to her parents and was isolated, all alone in her suffering.

What happened to her is completely understandable in terms of the neurobiology of traumatic encoding: a terrifying or threatening event, pre-existing emotional vulnerability, and a sense of inescapability.

A sexual assault is a profound threat to our survival, representing not just the physical violence but the annihilation of our sense of self and self-worth.

Mandy had a degree of pre-existing emotional vulnerability shown by her striving and need to excel. Emotional vulnerability is usually a pre-condition for trauma being hard-wired in the brain, unless the event itself is truly overwhelming. Some highly resilient people can suffer the same fate and not have long-lasting consequences.

Being powerless, helpless or trapped is another pre-condition of traumatic encoding – a defining feature of the experience of sexual assault. Victims of sexual abuse can be trapped over a long period of time, completely powerless.

So the conditions were laid for the trauma of sexual assault to be hard-wired in her brain together with the subconscious triggers that activate her emotional and stress reactions.

That's why the second sexual assault was more devastating. It re-triggered all the elements of the rape and now added another whole layer of inescapability. Her life fell apart.

Mandy now has put all of this behind her. After her course of self-healing therapy, she took time off college and found a job caring for others. She rebuilt her life and is now studying again.

Remarkably, she is now amazingly resilient. She told me about a very bad week with three very distressing life events, one after another - including crashing her car - but she bounced back immediately and told me how great her life was! I am deeply moved when I see this degree of resilience in my clients, following such profound vulnerability.

How did this miracle happen? She came for a five-day retreat of trauma practice, energy healing, life coaching, good food, pampering, long walks on the beach and connection to nature. In the course of the practice we erased the hard-wired trauma from her brain.

When all the emotional trauma was gone, we did a second round to clear the body imprint of the trauma – she was aware of a horrible feeling of restriction in her neck and wrists. These physical body reactions to trauma – sometimes including chronic pain – are also hard-wired as part of the trauma.

Importantly, she never had to tell me any of the details of the assaults, which would have been re-traumatising and might have felt shameful and humiliating. I simply asked her to briefly bring to mind her memory of the events, which activates the nerve circuits that hold the trauma. The process of healing was then gentle and effortless because of our in-built mechanism in the brain that permanently erases the layers of trauma. Later on, I explain the science of how that works.

We can use the same process with victims of physical abuse and neglect. I have a lot of clients who had one or more parents with alcoholism. In their childhood they were the victim of a parent's drunken rage, perhaps waiting scared each night for their father to come home from the bar and beat up their mother, or give them a walloping. In fact, children can be severely traumatised even if they are not directly hurt, just seeing their mother attacked is enough to leave emotional scars.

In this case, we use a similar process, deleting the memories of the violence and trauma, allowing the small child part in our memories to feel safe again.

Abandonment
Among my clients, a fear of abandonment is very common and it can have devastating effects on relationships. Often the feelings of abandonment arise from childhood experiences when you felt alone or your emotional needs weren't met. Perhaps your parents split up when you were small? Maybe your mother was in hospital for a long time and you

didn't know if she would ever come back?

Some people have feelings of abandonment because they were sent away to boarding school or another institution at an early age, where they were separated from their family. Others may have lost parents at an early age, through violence imprisonment, or illness.

This is not about blaming your parents; they were no doubt trying to be the best parents they could, with the resources they had. We all have some degree of trauma in our backgrounds. Just growing up presents a significant emotional challenge because we have to make the transition from being totally helpless and dependent on our parents as babies, to separating ourselves as independent adults.

All of these painful circumstances can cause a fear of abandonment to be hard-wired in your brain, leading to emotional over-reaction and many relationship difficulties.

I had major fears of abandonment for decades, mostly relating to one emotionally devastating event. My father was in the military and was posted to another country every two or three years. I never had a constant childhood home or friends and I attended many schools before I was ten. My education was very compromised so my parents made the difficult decision to send me to private boarding school, which they could hardly afford. I'm grateful for their action because otherwise I never would have completed my education and become a doctor. However, the emotional impact was long-lasting.

I have a vivid child-like memory of the moment my parents left me. I was standing in front of the school and the matron, a truly scary woman, had my hand in a tight grip. I was devastated, frightened and crying as my parents' car disappeared down the driveway. In fact the trauma is so intense that the memory is dissociated – I see the scene from a distance, like in a photograph. I am no longer in the body of the frightened ten year old. I think my parents also felt very distressed, leaving me there.

Author, age ten

For very many years, this intense fear of abandonment would rise up if I had even the slightest argument with my wife Meredith. It wasn't a realistic fear. Meredith is intensely loyal and has never threatened to leave me - but for me the fear was very real.

In my memory, I would rush to say sorry and beg forgiveness. Meredith actually had her own fears of abandonment so her memory is quite different. She would get confused and hurt because I wouldn't talk to her, I'd go hide in my cave.

It's a good illustration of how powerfully the encoded emotions can harm a loving relationship, and how it shaped our perceptions and memories in different ways.

These emotional reactions and difficulties meant that we couldn't easily resolve disputes because I couldn't express my feelings. Fortunately our arguments were few and far between, and we have a very happy and long-lasting marriage. Our relationship has deepened greatly as we have both healed our wounds.

My intense fear of abandonment was completely resolved in fifteen minutes of therapy by simply erasing the traumatic memory of the ten-year-old me. At the end of therapy I burst out laughing and the therapist asked me why.

My visual memory had changed in a delightful way, even though I still knew the objective facts of the event. In my mind, I was now inside the body of the ten-year-old me and I had all my power back. I suddenly and unexpectedly pulled my hand out of the grip of the matron, turned around, kicked her in the shin, and ran away!

I was no longer trapped, the trauma was relieved. From that day forward, my fear of abandonment was gone. On the rare occasions I am in dispute with Meredith, I can remain calm and we can work things out, both being able to state how we feel and what we need. Instead of reacting in a child-like way, I can respond as an adult.

In evolutionary terms, the fear of abandonment is very primitive – it's a threat to survival. Even small babies become distressed if they are separated from their mothers. This fear of abandonment is therefore very powerful and it can magnify the emotional reaction to ordinary upsets in a relationship.

Perhaps you just had an argument with your partner, who became angry. This can be enough to trigger overwhelming fears that the love you depend on will be withdrawn. So you tend to overreact in ways that are harmful to the relationship.

You might become overly submissive, always apologising for any argument or upset with your partner. Maybe you are too scared to speak up about something that bothers you. This means that issues can't get resolved and your partner doesn't have the opportunity to take responsibility for their side of the relationship.

Or else, you can start projecting your fears onto your partner so that their innocent actions then start to look like evidence of abandonment or lack of love. Your over-reaction is upsetting for your partner because it feels like you don't trust them. Over a period of time, this can seriously erode a relationship.

It may be that you have had a series of relationships where the same pattern developed, resulting in your partner breaking off the relationship – thereby reinforcing your fears. In the end, it becomes so painful that you develop a phobia about commitment, and you start unconsciously sabotaging each relationship. I see this pattern often and it all stems from this inbuilt, hard-wired fear of abandonment.

Fortunately, these feelings of abandonment that are the result of traumatic memories can easily be erased. If there is a long pattern of abandonment, you might have to tackle it, layer by layer, which takes more time. When the trauma is gone, the ordinary upsets that occur in any relationship no longer become threatening because your automatic and fearful emotional reaction is gone. You can remain calm and sort out the situation. You can make your own needs known and the relationship can be developed in a healthy and resilient way.

Betrayal
Being betrayed by someone we love is a devastating

experience. Our whole world can turn upside down. Everything we took for granted can suddenly be threatened. Some people never get over it and they remain bitter and distrustful all the rest of their life.

Like the fear of abandonment, betrayal stirs up our most primitive fears. In evolutionary terms, betrayal by the ones who love you is a life-threatening situation. When animals are expelled from the pack, they can be left starving and defenceless.

So the experience of betrayal sets the scene for a powerful traumatic memory, which can have lifetime consequences. Inescapability is one of the preconditions for hard-wiring emotional trauma and this is exactly what happens in betrayal. You can't escape the pain or hurt.

Having once been betrayed, it is very difficult to build trust again. Betrayal creates a hard-wired traumatic memory that reshapes your brain and all your perceptions, as well as your emotional reactions.

Your fears of betrayal may greatly compromise the development of a new relationship. When you are hypersensitive to this risk, you misinterpret ordinary events. You might become jealous of your partner's attention to someone else, when it's just an innocent friendship.

If you voice your concerns or get overly upset, your partner will start to feel you don't trust them. Over time, this pattern of interaction can gradually poison a relationship.

None of this is your fault. The emotional reactions you get are real, and not something you can just dismiss or talk your way out of. That's the thing about traumatic memories, they get programmed into the brain to create completely automatic emotional reactions so they become part of your operating system. No amount of reassurance from your partner can take away your subconscious fears.

You might have had a series of failed relationships where it seems, again and again, that you were betrayed by your partner. It's possible that your fear of betrayal, and the terrible pain it causes, may have led you subconsciously to sabotage relationships by suspecting your partner is being unfaithful.

Being betrayed is a terrible blow to your sense of self-worth. As your confidence is eroded, you become less and less able to construct healthy relationships where you can make known your own needs.

This cycle of failed relationships truly is a tragic consequence of your first experience of betrayal. Even though your reactions may have eroded or even destroyed subsequent relationships, it's ultimately not your fault.

Fortunately, the memory of betrayal can be erased. Like with abandonment, if there is a long history of betrayal you might have to take the time to work through the layers of betrayal, one by one. This process removes the trauma so that you don't react in the same fear-driven way to innocent events. You are able to build a new relationship built on mutual trust and to restore your sense of self-worth.

> **Erasing limiting beliefs and building self-worth**
>
> This is one of the most wonderful aspects of my practice, seeing clients radiate a new found self-worth and confidence, and holding these beliefs about their goodness with utter conviction. Having that sense of self-worth literally changes your whole world. When I witness that sudden shift in my clients, I feel like dancing with delight!
>
> This process of transformation has two elements: erasing the trauma and then building the positive – self-worth, confidence, kindness and generosity. Our deepest beliefs about ourselves are formed in early childhood – are we worthy, are we lovable, are we secure, are we safe? Research shows that the first three years of life powerfully predict what kind of person we become and how well we do in life. Fortunately, we now know these programs can be changed, and rapidly.

When our Windows PC computer crashes, it's usually caused by a corruption in the operating system, or a computer virus. To address the problem, we can restart Windows in 'Safe Mode' and then eliminate the bad code. We can do much the same in therapy, putting the brain into 'safe mode' and erasing the neural encoding that saps our self-worth or make us insecure in relationships. This safe mode of the brain is analogous to your brain state during deep sleep, which is a time of replenishment and healing, as well as consolidating new knowledge and beliefs into permanent memory.

Imagine what it means to truly believe, '*I am enough!*'

That changes everything. You no longer look to external things to secure your happiness because you already have enough; you can confidently assert yourself without worrying what other people think; you can build loving relationships where you make sure your own needs are met, as well as supporting your partner.

When you can leave abuse, abandonment, and betrayal behind, and grow into your full sense of self-worth, you are ready for the most beautiful friendships and love.

Being free to make good choices, you can bring the best parts of you to the world.

4. Losing Meaning in life

Many of my clients feel lost; they don't know what their purpose is in life. They find it very hard to gain a focus or commit to a sustained course of action. When you are immersed in stress and negative emotions, it's very hard to perceive your gifts and talents. You don't know how to make a meaningful contribution.

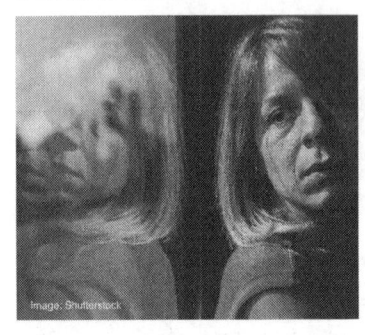

At worst, those who have suffered major trauma can feel worthless, abandoned by their God. You might even believe that you deserve to suffer, that you are unable to give love to others.

The truth is, we are born as innocent souls, deeply connected to the Universe and all things. New babies do not know they are in any way separate from everything they perceive. They are pure subjectivity, just a mass of feelings. It takes time for a baby to begin to realize that people and objects are outside and separate. Over time, we develop this sense of separation and objectivity. Being separate, we develop fears, anxieties and the need for ego defences.

Our ego is most active when we are ruminating on matters, worrying about our status, our relationships, our future, or feeling dissatisfied with the past. When our emotional needs are not met early in life, the ego creates a variety of personality traits (called 'protector roles') to shield us from the pain of the wounded, inner child. Typical ego protector roles include: intellectualizing everything, or becoming super competent, or always being critical so it's always somebody else's fault, or adopting angry roles that lash out at everyone, or adopting a victim role. Underlying these different parts of our personality is our true compassionate self, which can be hard to access when we are busy activating all our ego defences.

The part of the brain associated with the ego, which lights up when we are stuck in self-rumination, is called the 'default mode network'. In contrast, when we are caught up in the moment, fully engaged in an enjoyable or absorbing activity, the default mode network switches off. We forget about ourselves.

Curiously, neuroscientists have also found that suppression of this default mode network correlates with deeply meaningful experiences during psychedelic trips. Under the right conditions, many people report a life-changing experience of deep spiritual connection to the Universe, of pure subjectivity, of not being separate from anything. This state is joyful and awe inspiring.

Therefore the deepest meaning in life arises when

we forget our ego concerns, and bring our greatest gifts and talents in service to others.

In my experience, as my clients leave behind their trauma and re-discover their true sense of worth, they find much deeper meaning in life. They create positive relationships, engage fully in worthwhile activities, and broaden their perception to experience what's good and meaningful in life.

While the self-healing practice I use to release trauma is rooted very firmly in science, the process involves a deep and sacred connection, conveyed with a healing intention and very specific forms of soothing touch. The work is intuitive and almost effortless for both therapist and client.

The experience of this intimate connection creates meaning for my clients and inspires them to deepen their own connections. Indeed, a number of my clients were so inspired by their healing experience that they have chosen to train in the modality and become practitioners themselves!

5. Hindering your Accomplishments

Happiness is not just found in activities in the present moment; it also stems from reflection on a life well lived, on meaningful contributions and accomplishments in the world. When you can look back and say, '*I made a positive difference*,' when your hard work is rewarded by new skills or qualifications, when your children grow up to be good citizens, when you build something worthwhile or beautiful – all these are sources of long-lasting happiness.

Emotional trauma can paralyse your ability to progress achievements. Accomplishments require engagement in a task or project and we have already explored how engagement is inhibited by self-criticism, fear of failure and lack of confidence. Often limiting beliefs get in the way, '*I am not good enough*,' or '*I don't deserve this*,' are beliefs that will stop you from apply for a course, reaching out for a better job, or forming a relationship with someone you admire.

Emotional trauma causes chronic stress, which directly impairs your ability to learn and achieve. If you are chronically anxious, your sensory and perceptual systems are closed right down to focus only on potential risk. Higher brain functions – in the cortex – go offline. So your ability to focus on a new task, to understand and learn new concepts, to think clearly and to make up your mind, are all greatly impaired.

In addition, emotional trauma and chronic stress directly impact on your physical health, impair your sleep, cause chronic pain and addictions, and make you feel exhausted. Just surviving from day to day is all you can manage.

What is so wonderful to see in my clients, is how their talents and abilities are unleashed when the trauma and chronic stress are erased. One client who presented with severe PTSD and chronic pain has now just completed her Master's degree and is a new mother! Another client, who three years ago was bed-bound with severe chronic pain and disability, is now applying to do a Bachelor's degree in nursing.

When you put it all together, it makes complete sense why we can struggle so much, and why trauma makes us unhappy.

But you CAN heal the trauma and release the chains that hold you back. Now it's time to learn about the amazing scientific discovery that underpins this new understanding of self-healing.

4. THE SCIENCE BEHIND THIS PRACTICE

At the beginning of this book, I explained how emotional trauma becomes hard-wired in the brain, driving automatic emotional, body and stress reactions. Although many forms of therapy refer to 'changing the wiring in your brain' or activating 'neural plasticity' (which really means the same thing), the practice I use is unique in having a detailed scientific theory and molecular mechanism of action.

The science and practice is known as Havening Techniques®. The word 'haven' means a safe place. 'Havening' is the transitive verb, meaning to take someone to a safe place – the opposite of trauma.

Ronald Ruden MD

The brilliant research scientist

who developed Havening is a medical doctor in the USA, the partner of a successful medical practice in New York. Dr Ronald Ruden has spent nearly twenty years researching and refining the scientific theory and practice of this remarkable self-healing method. In a recent publication in Science Direct, he laid out the complete anatomical and molecular pathway for how trauma gets encoded in the brain and how to activate the self-healing mechanism[1]. For those with a science background, you might like to read the open access article here: https://doi.org/10.1016/j.explore.2018.05.005

In my opinion, Havening is one of the most astonishing medical breakthroughs in my lifetime and I have recently quit my career as a senior hospital doctor to focus full time on Havening practice, training and research.

> **What we know about the neuroscience**
> Thanks to Dr Ruden's research, I can tell you precisely how trauma gets stored in the brain. We know the sub-nuclei in the amygdala where this happens, the nerve pathways, neurotransmitters, receptors, cellular mechanisms, enzymes, and electrical signals that allow trauma to be encoded. We also know the pathways by which this encoded trauma affects our thinking, our perceptions, our emotions, our body functions, and stress reactions.

The extraordinary scientific discovery behind this

technique is that the mechanism for encoding trauma can be set in reverse. Dr Ruden has shown how to create the conditions where the nerve connections that encode the trauma can be severed in a matter of minutes, using the simple and gentle Havening Techniques.

How Havening Techniques are performed

The practice is usually done with the client sitting in a chair, fully clothed. Either the clients are guided to perform the specific forms of touch to themselves, or the touch is applied by the practitioner. In that case, the practitioner usually sits to the side of the client so that he or she doesn't feel trapped or controlled.

Guided by the results from the neuroscience lab, we apply soothing touch by stroking the palms of the hands, the upper arms and the face. Specialised cells in these areas generate high levels of nerve signals that are connected to emotional centres in the brain[2]. Other areas of the skin don't have the same sensitivity[3].

Within twenty or thirty seconds of applying Havening touch, high levels of Delta Waves appear in the brain. These are the slowest type of brain waves, the opposite of the high-frequency waves that occur during trauma.

In general, the practitioner will make a careful assessment of the client to uncover where trauma might lie. Using a variety of techniques to deal with painful memories, difficult emotions, or stressful body reactions, the practitioner will briefly activate the trauma and then allow it to heal itself by creating safety with the Havening touch.

Applying the science

The practitioner uses knowledge of the science to interpret the client's reactions, and the changes in physiology, as the trauma is activated and the healing progresses. We have a detailed understanding of what is happening inside the client.

We can describe the electrical signals, neurotransmitters, receptors, and enzymes that remove glutamate receptors from the surface of neural cells, thus breaking the nerve connections and erasing the trauma. Moreover, we know the physiology of the unique sensory system that allows us to put the brain in 'safe mode' to delete the trauma and banish self-limiting beliefs[2,3].

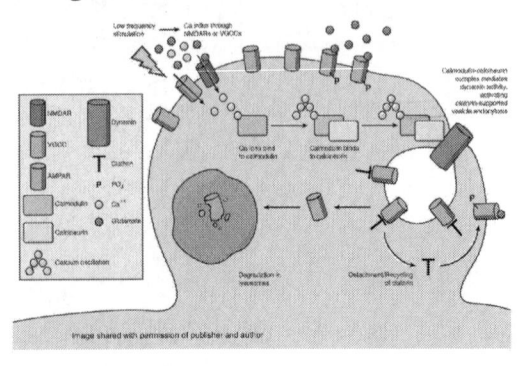

I have my own brain wave monitor – connected to an App on my iPhone – that allows me to monitor the spectrum of brain wave frequencies in my brain in real time. Within 20-30 seconds of applying Havening Touch to myself, I see a radical shift in my brain frequencies. As a doctor, I was so amazed to witness this for the first time, I nearly fell off my chair!

This detailed scientific theory and mechanism sets Havening apart from any other psychological therapy. Most therapies are empirical: we know they work but we have no idea how. Havening is different.

As a doctor, I was extremely sceptical of the claims of Havening. A close friend and admired colleague tried for two years to persuade me to do the training and I refused. In medical terms, there is little 'evidence' that the therapy works. By that I mean, at the time of first drafting this book, there were no well-designed clinical trials published in peer-review medical journals, to prove the outcomes for patients. So if your doctor has even heard of Havening, he will probably be dismissive and tell you that Havening is not 'evidence-based'.

This is always the way with genuine scientific and medical breakthroughs, it can take years or even decades for new treatments to become established. So far, there are only a handful of my medical colleagues in the world, trained and certified in Havening Techniques, and so we are the pioneers.

Despite my own scepticism, I became curious when I read the outline of the scientific theory behind Havening. Then I found a video of one of the founders of Havening doing a 15-minute session to cure a major phobia in a client. The video shows the client re-visiting the source of her phobia and being astonished to find that all her fear had completely vanished. I too was extremely surprised.

I then tried an experiment. I rewound the video and inserted my own traumatic memory into the process. For fifteen minutes I simply copied the process to activate my own self-healing and was astounded to find that my traumatic memory was erased! I immediately signed up for the next Havening training and booked my airfares.

In this updated edition of my book, I'm thrilled to report that the first major, randomised, controlled, multi-centre trial of Havening has just been published in the Journal of Psychophysiology.

Kirsty Hodgson and Debbie Clayton from the Metropolitan University of Cardiff teamed up with Havening practitioners across England to identify one hundred twenty-five clients with Type D personality and test the outcomes of Havening[4].

Type D Personality describes those who have habitually negative feelings accompanied by social inhibition. This personality type has long been associated with much higher risks of chronic physical and mental illness, compared with the average population.

Painful emotions and lack of social connection cause chronic stress, which is accompanied by increased circulating stress hormones, such as cortisol, and raised blood pressure. Chronic stress increases your risk of heart disease and stroke, impairs your immune system, and can precipitate mental illness.

People with Type D personality are also more likely to live an unhealthy lifestyle, avoid health-sustaining activities and neglect their adherence to medication.

This personality type is usually the result of adverse experiences and emotional trauma early in life, affecting up to 30% of the population.

However, this breakthrough study showed that a single session of Havening Techniques greatly reduced the signs of Type D personality and significantly reduced cortisol and blood pressure.

Remarkably, the early response measured at 24 hours became even more pronounced one month after treatment. Prior to the treatment, 59 out of 68 participants who received Havening were classified as Type D personality. At one month, only 9 participants met the score for this diagnosis.

In contrast, the randomly matched control group of

57 subjects who did not receive Havening showed no change in their personality rating.

The implications of this study are profound. It overturns the dogma that personality types are stable over a lifetime and cannot be modified. The blood pressure response at one month after treatment was about as big as doctors would expect from starting first-line drug treatment for hypertension.

The persistent reduction in blood pressure and cortisol levels shows that chronic stress is diminished and long-term health risks are possibly reduced – from just one hour of simple and gentle treatment.

We will need long-term follow-up studies to prove the impact on physical health outcomes. However, practical experience suggests that personality changes and reduced stress responses after Havening are permanent.

An earlier, non-randomised trial of one session of Havening showed clinically significant improvements in depression, anxiety and work/social adjustment one week and two months after the Havening intervention[5].

What I, and hundreds of other practitioners, observe in our practice completely correlates with the scientific theory. The therapy is based on the science so we can precisely target our interventions.

The scientific theory predicts that the molecular mechanism that erases trauma is active for about 5-7 minutes. Many times, I have seen traumatic memories simply disappear within that time frame. For most clients, we repeat the process several times until all of the trauma is erased, typically taking 15-20 minutes in total.

Here's one illustration. A client, in her sixties, presented with a serious earthquake phobia. She lived in a city that was destroyed in an earthquake. Hundreds of people died and many thousands were injured. About 80% of the central city buildings were ultimately demolished. My client lived through horror of the earthquake and for eight years had lived with daily anxiety, hyper-vigilance and frequent fear responses. Any slight shaking would trigger her reaction.

There were many places she couldn't drive a car because it felt unsafe – such as tunnels, or roads near fault lines. Earthquakes are especially traumatising because they don't just happen once, the main shock is followed by hundreds of after-shocks, all of which are potentially deadly.

Given my knowledge of the science of trauma, I did some detective work to find out when the trauma was encoded in her brain, which is not necessarily at the time of the major trauma. When I asked if she ever had '*this kind of fear before*' she realised that the major earthquake was not her first experience of this frightening event. She'd witnessed one as a teenager, some fifty years before, which she described as '*very frightening, actually quite traumatising.*'

In less than five minutes of therapy, she completely erased the trauma of her teen experience. I saw the sudden change in her, as if the fear fell out of her. She appeared completely surprised, looked under her chair and around the room and said, '*Where did it go?!!!*'

When I asked her to recall the early life earthquake, she could recall the facts of the event but was completely unable to connect to any of the fear. All she could remember was being safe. Then I asked her to remember the very traumatic event of the big earthquake in the city where she lived and she looked so puzzled – she just couldn't feel the fear any more!

By chance, we were on the phone about a month later. I asked her how '*the earthquake thing was going?*'

'*Oh,*' she exclaimed, '*I had completely forgotten about it!*' I then heard a sharp intake of breath as she recalled with amazement that, the previous weekend, she had joined friends for a picnic in a beauty spot that was accessed by driving through her most feared tunnel. '*I didn't even think about it!*' she said.

I see this kind of reaction time after time in my clinic – astonishment and laughter because trauma that has weighed so heavily on peoples' lives is suddenly lifted, as if by magic.

What I want to emphasise at this point is that Havening Techniques is a *self-healing* process. I am not *doing* therapy to my clients, I am using my healing intention and presence, scientific knowledge and skills to create the optimal conditions for healing to occur. The client does the healing, not me. This is a radically different paradigm from mainstream medical practice.

This is why this practice is so amazingly life-changing. Imagine if you could release your burden of negative emotions and stress. Suppose you could throw yourself into meaningful and enjoyable engagement with excitement and confidence. How would it be to have secure and loving relationships? What if you could find your true meaning and purpose in life? Imagine what exciting accomplishments would be possible.

You will also be equipped with new tools for self-healing so that you are better prepared to cope with life stresses and to sustain your wellbeing. I am so delighted to see how resilient my clients become.

I had these words from a client today:

'*I have never in my life not been nervous for a new*

job. I started last week with confidence and not caring what people thought of me, which is absolutely massive for me. But overall, given I'm still processing a recent breakup, my parents have just separated and I'm in a new job, I think I'm doing remarkably well. I wouldn't be feeling like this a year ago!'

When I speak of rapid results, I want to put that in context. Most clients with these kinds of life-long life struggles attend counselling, psychotherapy or clinical psychology for months or years. Most see an improvement, some are healed enough to get back to their lives, and some make little or no progress.

With Havening Techniques, most of my clients leave the first session feeling very different. They are amazed that a painful traumatic memory has been completely erased. Or a great burden of negative emotions has been lifted so the feeling of overwhelm is replaced by calm.

Some clients in life crisis come for a personal five-day residential healing retreat where they receive daily Havening, life coaching, nourishing food, connection to nature, and time for personal reflection. What I witness is a radical shift in life trajectory, with new perspectives on life, leaving the traumatic past behind, and stepping forward with positivity and resilience.

Part of the professional approach is doing a very careful assessment of the emotional vulnerability of each client, and finding out how deeply rooted and complex the trauma may be.

Some clients are generally resilient and have just isolated events of trauma they want to leave behind, such as my client with the car crash. Others have more complex, early life trauma thus much more work is required to skilfully guide the client through a healing journey. Erasing trauma is not the end of the work – we then want to build strengths, positive self-beliefs, and life skills so that the client becomes resilient, self-confident and vibrant.

A small minority of clients have very severe and complex trauma and we have to patiently unpick the layers over a longer period of time. What they see is sustained progress, a lifting of life's burdens, and hugely significant improvements in their ability to meet challenging circumstances. Things that were triggering no longer affect them; they have increasing periods of time without anxiety; they experience a re-connection to life and an increasing sense of self-worth and capability.

Dr Ronald Ruden has become a colleague and personal friend. I now make it my life's mission to spread news of this remarkable healing practice around the world, especially among my medical colleagues who have never heard of it.

At medical school, they don't teach you about self-healing in patients! This practice is very new and the very first training course was only in 2013. I have become one of only thirty or so Certified

Havening Trainers in the world. I'm delighted that more and more doctors are now coming to my training courses.

Next steps

Let's recap the material we've covered so far. I want us all to be on the same page:

- You are not alone in your life struggles – so many others grapple with the same problems
- Your life struggles are not your fault
- Programmed brain reactions – from early life – are undermining your happiness and your ability to accomplish things in life
- The amazing new science shows that we all have a built-in mechanism to rapidly delete trauma
- When our trauma is deleted, we are freed from the past and can now shine as the best version of ourselves
- The healing practices that enable this transformation are called Havening Techniques
- You do the healing yourself, under the guidance of a qualified practitioner
- You also learn techniques for self-therapy, to enhance your resilience and wellbeing

How big an impact might Havening make on the world? My personal view is that we are at the start of a revolution, not just because emotional trauma is so commonplace but also because many physical illnesses have their origin in chronic stress.

Science References

1. Ruden R A(2019) Harnessing Electroceuticals to Treat Disorders Arising From Traumatic Stress: Theoretical Considerations Using A Psychosensory Model. Explore 15(3):222-229.

2. Vrontou S, Wong A M, Rau K K, Koerber H R, Anderson D J (2013) Genetic identification of C-fibers that detect massage-like stroking of hairy skin in vivo. Nature 493(7434): 669–673

3. Harper M (2012) Taming the Amygdala: An EEG Analysis of Exposure Therapy for the Traumatized. Traumatology
18(2): 61–74

4. Hodgson K, Clayton D, Carmi M, Carmi L, Ruden R, Fraser W, Cameron D (2020) A Psychophysiological Examination of the Mutability of Type D Personality in a Therapeutic Trial. Journal of Psychophysiology. Published online 2nd September: https://doi.org/10.1016/j.explore.2018.05.005

5. Thandi G, Tom D, Gould M, McKenna P, Greenberg N (2015) Impact of a Single-Session of Havening. Health Science Journal Vol.9 No 5:1: 1-5

5. THE COMMUNITY IMPACT OF TRAUMA

Emotional trauma often starts early in life. Babies in utero are sensitive to the emotional wellbeing of their mother. If the mother has chronic anxiety, the growing baby is bathed in stress hormones and is likely to be born with a heightened degree of emotional vulnerability.

Birth trauma can also directly impact on the emotional wellbeing of a child. Birth asphyxia – breathing difficulties – and the necessary medical resuscitation procedures can lead to lifelong anxiety disorders.

However, the greatest impact seems to occur during our formative years as small children. A great deal of research has focussed on this area and the results are deeply concerning.

The Adverse Childhood Experiences (ACE)

studies

Emotional trauma and abuse in childhood dramatically impacts adult health and wellbeing. Adverse childhood experiences (ACE) are defined as:

- emotional abuse
- physical abuse
- sexual abuse
- witnessing a mother being treated violently
- household substance abuse
- household mental illness
- parental separation or divorce
- a family member in prison
- emotional neglect
- physical neglect

Many children have multiple risk factors and the ACE score for an individual child is the number of adverse experiences from the above list. For instance, a person who was a victim of physical abuse, who witnessed domestic violence and whose parents separated would have an ACE score of 3.

Multiple studies have shown that having a high ACE score dramatically increases the risk of a wide range of health problems later in life: alcoholism, chronic lung disease, depression, illegal drug use, alcohol abuse, coronary heart disease, liver disease, sexually transmitted diseases, smoking, suicide attempts, teen pregnancy, and sexual violence.

For instance, a study from the WAVE Trust in the UK (https://www.wavetrust.org/what-are-adverse-childhood-experiences) showed that those with an ACE score of four and above have:

- 3x the rate of smoking and chronic lung disease
- 11x the rate of intravenous drug abuse
- 14x the number of suicide attempts
- 4.5x the rate of depression
- 2x the rate of liver disease

Those with six or more ACE's have an average life expectancy 20 years less than those with ACE score of zero.

ACE's are not uncommon. Two thirds of the UK population has at least one ACE. One in eight people have four or more ACE's. We are witnessing a crisis of mental health, especially in our young people.

A note of caution is warranted here. Not every adverse experience becomes a trauma. Some people are naturally resilient and can leave difficult experiences behind them, without being traumatised, even in childhood. If you had good-enough parents in a stable relationship, you are unlikely to be significantly traumatised.

Furthermore, the authors of the original study on Adverse Childhood Experiences caution that the score is not predictive for individuals. A child who had a high intensity or duration of one adverse experience, such as repeated physical abuse, may be at much higher risk than those with a higher ACE score.

On a population-wide basis, emotional trauma does create a huge burden of mental health problems, addictions and chronic physical illness. Unfortunately, early life trauma makes you much more susceptible to being re-traumatised as an adult. Many of my clients have layers and layers of trauma.

Adverse child experiences are also strongly correlated with subsequent violence and criminality. The Prisoner ACE Study from Bangor University in Wales (https://www.bangor.ac.uk/news/documents/PHW-Prisoner-ACE-Survey-Report-E.pdf) found that nearly half of the adult prisoners had four or more ACE's and eight out of ten reported at least one ACE.

Compared with prisoners with no ACE's, those with four or more ACE's were
- 3x more likely to have ever been convicted of criminal damage
- 3x more likely to have ever been convicted of violence against the person
- 3x more likely to have ever been convicted of theft
- 2x more likely to have ever been convicted of drugs offences

Trauma-informed programs among prisoners and

perpetrators of domestic violence show promise in reducing rates of reoffending. This is a whole new area where Havening Techniques might make a huge impact. Wouldn't it be wonderful to break the endless cycle of inter-generational violence?

Havening Techniques not only promise a revolution in mental health and the treatment of addiction, they also have a potentially huge impact on our physical health as well.

Many patients present to their family doctor or to hospital specialists with illnesses for which there is limited medical therapy: chronic back pain, muscle aches and fibromyalgia, neuralgia, chronic pelvic pain, bowel complaints, migraines, chemical sensitivities and allergies, persistent rashes, neurological symptoms for which no cause can be found, and so on.

I have seen some of my clients cure or dramatically improved drug allergies, chronic pain, severe skin rashes, gut problems, neuralgia, and even partial paralysis. All these effects are explainable in terms of the science of traumatic encoding. Unfortunately, most doctors are not yet trained in the science of trauma. They are often frustrated with patients who keep coming back with problems that they don't know how to treat.

We also know that chronic trauma, stress and pessimism is potentially lethal. For instance a huge study that followed people for many years after a heart attack found that pessimists had a death rate four times higher than optimists.

The American Stress Institute documents the many physical problems that result from chronic stress: headaches, depression, insomnia, weakened immune function, raised blood sugar, hypertension, risk of heart attack, stomach ache, tense muscles, fertility problems, missed periods and erectile dysfunction.

To that we might add all the unhealthy stress-related behaviours such as over-eating, excess alcohol consumption, smoking, and illegal drug use.

When combined with chronic anxiety and depression, all these conditions add up to about 80% of the workload of family doctors.

In my experience, when the underlying trauma is treated, then many of the chronic health problems and addictions start to fade away.

In view of the enormous community burden of trauma, we urgently need to promote effective methods of healing, of which Havening Techniques seems by far the most promising.

Doctors may well be sceptical of this claim. However, as a medical specialist, and former international leader in healthcare quality and safety, I can say that my own observation of client outcomes is strong evidence that Havening is powerfully effective, and what I witness precisely aligns with the scientific theory.

The recently published randomised, controlled trial (RCT) of Havening – mentioned in the last chapter – confirms that objective measures of chronic health risk, such as hypertension and raised cortisol levels, are persistently reduced after just one session of Havening.

So I hope this little book has helped you understand how emotional trauma can impact on your life, how many of your life difficulties are understandable – and not your fault! The exciting news is that we now have a powerful self-healing mechanism to release our trauma and begin to live happy and meaningful lives.

While healing your own wounds is your first priority, the implications of this new healing method are much wider. It's a pathway into building a better world.

6. MAKING A PERSONAL COMMITMENT

There comes a point in life when our inner being screams 'Enough!' and we make a personal commitment to change.

This book is for you, at this moment of choice.

Maybe you are just stuck in life, repeating the same patterns over and over again? Or life is such a struggle that you barely get by. You feel empty and depressed, as if you've lost all purpose.

You're working so hard to get ahead but even your accomplishments feel hollow. You're chronically stressed and anxious.

Perhaps you are sad and lonely, filled with heartache? You wonder why you choose partners who treat you badly and you begin to think, *'Maybe I don't deserve love?'* Your self-worth is at an all time low.

It's not just our personal lives that cause us distress. It seems the world is going crazy and we want to shout, '*Stop! There has to be a better way!*'

Endless violence, greed and environmental destruction is killing us all. What kind of a world are we creating for our children? How do we even begin to address problems that seem so overwhelming?

The one thing that links all these scenarios is a sense of powerlessness. Even if you know better ways of living, you find finding yourself stuck in the rut. You have gifts and talents to offer the world but you can't seem to get started.

Deep down, you know you have a purpose in life and you just ache to live a meaningful life and to fulfill your calling.

Now, through reading this book, you know how the trauma that holds you back can be erased. Equipped with positive emotions, meaningful engagement, and healthy relationships, you are ready to accomplish great things in life.

Imagine the possibility of turning your whole life around in just a few months – or even in one week.

Don't just do it for you, do it for the world. Heal yourself and you start to heal your loved ones and the wider world in ways that are far more powerful than you can imagine.

I share these life lessons in my TEDx talk, '*Perfectly broken and ready to heal*' (https://youtu.be/jTYS-zLtbYTU). I tell the story of how I campaigned for more than a decade, all around the world, to bring more humanity and compassion to healthcare. For many years my message met with resistance but when I changed my own attitudes and beliefs the world started to listen.

Here's why your personal commitment to change can have such a powerful impact on the world.

The world 'out there' is an illusion

In our Western culture, we're conditioned to objectify people and things and see them as separate from us. Thus the external world appears to takes on a concrete reality, which we feel powerless to change.

But the truth is very different. Most of what we see 'out there' is powerfully shaped by our perceptions and beliefs; it's just a story we are telling ourselves. When we shift our own attitudes and beliefs, the world changes around us in powerful ways.

An example is those who fall into the role of the victim. They believe their lives are 'ruined' because their parents didn't love them enough, or they were abandoned or abused. They feel the world owes them something. Every one of their relationships is based on resentment and neediness.

Their lives are full of drama and conflict. Often they have family or friends who continually rescue them, which only reinforces their helpless, victim role.

People who are caught in this trap project their beliefs onto the world and so become victims again and again; the world obliges by fulfilling their expectations. They feel helplessly trapped in this cycle of misery. It's a painful place to be; I wouldn't like to live inside their heads.

Yet their whole world changes overnight when they choose to take responsibility for their own lives, when they stop blaming and instead focus on what they could contribute. Instead of obsessing about themselves, they start to become aware of the needs of others. It can start with small acts of kindness, or helping people in the community, or focusing on gratitude rather than resentment.

Now the world that seemed so unfair becomes much more kind and friendly. Instead of being trapped in powerlessness, the former victims now have many positive choices.

This is just one example of how our world reality can be radically changed by something as simple as changing our attitude. However, while the shift may be simple in theory, the process of change may be very painful. It's hard to come to the realization that your own actions are causing so much pain in the world. Taking responsibility for your own feelings, rather than blaming them on others, is a really big step in personal growth.

With our new understanding of emotional trauma, we can be more compassionate towards the person who falls into the victim role. Imagine how much easier this person could grow and change if all their past trauma was erased?

In using this example, I'm not suggesting that you are taking on the victim role; it's simply an illustration of how powerfully the way we show up in our lives, changes the world around us.

Here's another example of how the world can change when we change ourselves. Imagine two different workplaces: one that drives you to exhaustion and burnout; and another where you absolutely love your work. Here's a story of people who shifted from one reality to another – without even having to change their job!

I've worked for a lifetime in healthcare. The surveys show that about 30% to 50% of my fellow health professionals have symptoms of burnout, characterized by emotional exhaustion, depersonalization and cynicism.

Many health workers spend a great deal of time thinking about how tired and stressed they are, how they hate their jobs and their bosses, and how demanding and ungrateful the patients are – they are relentlessly bringing their attention to the negative aspects of their work.

This state of burnout is the end result of a medical system that brutalizes and dehumanizes many who work in the caring professions. I could tell you horrifying tales from my own training, such as my first weekend on duty as a junior doctor. I worked nonstop from Saturday morning until Monday evening with only three hours' sleep. I ran from crisis to crisis, feeling completely overwhelmed and frightened. Six of my patients died, despite all my efforts to save them. Horrors like that can scar you for life.

Sadly, the traumatization of health professionals tends to get propagated through the generations. Those who were abused and dehumanized early in their career had to 'toughen up' and then become the harsh mentors to new generations of young graduates.

No wonder our young doctors and nurse get brutalized! But some remarkable individuals transcend all that suffering and find ways to truly *love* their jobs. I've interviewed many such health professionals to learn their secrets. Many of them were burnt out at some stage. What happened to shift their reality?

Universally, they make a conscious decision to direct more of their attention to the good things in their work. Instead of ruminating on the frustrations of their workplace, they deliberately reflect on the privilege of the intimate human connection they experience with patients each day. They focus on kindness, compassion and caring and not just the technical aspects of their job. They find inspiration in the courage and resilience of their patients.

In turn, these doctor and nurses experience a world that is much kinder to them. Their patients are more grateful and less demanding. Their workmates greet them with a smile rather than a frown. Their work days are less stressed and hurried and their patients recover more quickly.

Shifting from being a victim to being responsible, or from hating your job to loving it, depends on your power to make personal choices. Erase your trauma, let go of your fears, and suddenly you are ready to start inspiring positive change in the world.

Opportunities open up that you could never see before. The ripple effects are amazing and you quickly become a positive influence in so many other lives.

Is it time for you to make a personal commitment to this change?

The possibilities don't end there. What if the natural world also has remarkable self-healing powers? What if the climate crisis and environmental collapse could also be addressed far more effectively by supporting processes of natural self-healing, rather than trying to apply technological fixes?

Witnessing the miraculous changes in my clients has radically shifted my beliefs about what is possible in the natural world. The intimacy of connection I experience during my healing practice has shown me the possibility of a very different relationship between humankind and the world we inhabit.

At this time of crisis in the world, I invite you to consider new ways of healing the world. In the next chapter I share how my philosophies of practice have shaped my worldview.

7. MY PHILOSOPHY OF PRACTICE

I live in the small town of Raglan on the west coast of the North Island of New Zealand. Raglan has been voted one of the most beautiful towns in NZ, sited on a lovely harbour, with the ocean and beaches just minutes away. It's our spiritual home.

I share my life with my beloved wife Meredith and we have been together for over forty years. Meredith is an energy healer, a mentor, and is well known in our community for her hosting, baking and cooking. We have a studio apartment in our home, which is a peaceful retreat for family and friends, and those struggling with life challenges. We like nothing better than to invite people into our home and help them set a completely new direction in life.

The Coronavirus pandemic has imposed social-distancing on many communities and so we have missed the healing connection of human touch. During that time, I offered my practice by online video connection, where the client does their own soothing touch guided by me. Although this online practice can be remarkably effective, I don't think it can compare to hands-on practice and deep healing connection.

I know from scientific studies, and my own experience, how intimately people are connected when they are physically close together. As a doctor, I learned that my personal presence could be agitating or healing for my patients. Thus I was very careful to bring a calm, soothing, compassionate and healing energy to each patient encounter, and that helped develop rapport and trust.

A compassionate presence has a remarkable effect on the healing and recovery of patients, as shown by many research studies. If you have a compassionate doctor, you will experience less anxiety and pain, you will recover from more quickly from injury, surgery, or illness, and if you have advanced cancer your survival will be prolonged.

When engaging with others, we are alert to subtle changes in their facial expression, tone of voice, body posture, and even chemical signals – all of which mean that practitioner and client are intimately connected. During my Havening practice, I am exquisitely attuned to the subtle changes in my clients and those signals shape my intuition and guidance.

Many of these forms of connection are missing in

a video communication. That explains why we become so exhausted with endless Zoom meetings and other forms of online connection, because we are having to work so hard to overcome the limits to human communication.

Many of us have developed 'Zoom fatigue' during the Coronavirus outbreak and we long for real human connection. I find myself bombarded with offers of online programs and events and now I just want to delete them all.

When I practice online with clients in remote locations, after a few sessions I begin to feel fatigued and mildly stressed. I know that my clients are not getting the full benefit of what I can offer. For clients, doing Havening touch to oneself is not as powerful as having another human being offer you loving, healing touch.

However, when I practice in person with my client in the room, I am completely relaxed and the sessions are energising for me. My energy affects my clients. So, at the end of in-person sessions, my clients are calm and safely contained, even if we have been dealing with painful life events and feelings. Their burden of negative feelings is lifted and their self-beliefs become more positive.

My clinic room is a haven, a place of healing. It is warm and welcoming, full of hand-crafted furnishings and objects, lovingly curated art, and items that have stories or represent spiritual connections for me.

There is another important reason for choosing to emphasise the importance of genuine human connection. Our civilisation faces multiple crises including climate change, environmental collapse, violence, social injustice, and epidemics of mental health problems and chronic illness. We have a sick society.

Meanwhile the big corporations and tech companies are rushing us into a dystopian future of video screens, virtual jobs, virtual relationships, virtual education and virtual lives.

All these media channels bombard us with sensationalist content and mass advertising, while manipulating our feelings to make us feel insecure. Our worth has become measured in Facebook 'likes' and numbers of virtual followers rather than real relationships.

The corporations pursue these deliberate strategies to persuade us that online browsing and buying material goods will make us happy, and thus increase their advertising revenue. This way of living our lives is catastrophic for our happiness and well-being, and for the planet we live on.

The only answer to these multiple crises is deep and meaningful connection – to truly connect to each other as human beings, to live in a real community, to connect to nature and the living planet.

Thus, I have made the personal decision to largely limit my practice to in-person work in my own clinic. The experience of the Coronavirus pandemic has only strengthened my commitment to serving the world through building human connection and healing.

I make one exception to my rule of in-person practice: if you are relatively resilient and have an isolated traumatic event that affects you, I am very happy to offer a single online session. The practice is powerful enough to permanently delete your traumatic memory and free you from the past.

How I practice

I believe that every human being has deep healing potential and this has been proven to me in client after client. Many people come to me with years of struggle; they have tried every kind of therapy and not made much progress. Some have little faith that Havening will be any different. But you don't have to believe in Havening for it to work. Indeed, I rather like having sceptical clients because their astonishment is even greater!

So, no matter how profound is your trauma, I hold deep faith that you can find your way to healing.

I tell every client, '*You have an amazing, intuitive, healing wisdom, which will guide your healing journey. This wisdom will control the pace and direction of your healing journey in a way that will always keep you safe. My job is to create the conditions to allow your healing to unfold, to hold a powerful healing intention, and to pay exquisite attention to what is arising.'*

To find healing from your trauma, you need to be briefly conscious of your trauma while at the same time having a deep feeling of safety, which neutralises the trauma. That is the origin of the word, 'Havening'. It means to take someone to a place of safety.

Many clients do not know the origin of their trauma. Early life events are not held in conscious memory but they can still profoundly affect us. Even as adults, we tend to bury very painful memories in our subconscious, when events are deeply traumatising.

So my job is to be your guide, using my knowledge and experience to navigate through your stories, feelings and body reactions to find the critical points in your life story where we can release the trauma.

One thing I want to emphasise again, I never need to hear the stories of your worst trauma. I would hate for you to be re-traumatised in telling the story of the awful things that happened to you. I don't need to know any of the details in order to help you erase the trauma.

I am a Certified Havening Trainer, one of only about

7. MY PHILOSOPHY OF PRACTICE

thirty in the world. I love training and coaching my students, helping them to be skilled in connecting with their clients, building trust, navigating the complexities of trauma, carefully observing their clients and knowing which techniques to apply. There is an art to this practice as well as a science.

I find the work energising. At the end of a full clinic, I am more energised than at the beginning of the day. I sit in awe and gratitude. I have a smile on my face and feel a warm glow inside me for hours after my clinic is finished. This is the most gratifying work I have ever done as a doctor.

I just love meeting new clients, knowing I have something very special and life-giving to offer. As I begin to explain about the science of emotional trauma and Havening, and tell the stories of lives I have seen transformed, I see tears in their eyes. Suddenly, their lifelong struggles become understandable, they see hope for the future. In that moment the healing begins.

Even though I give each client my full attention, I am not doing the work of healing. You are healing yourself in a gentle and easy process. When we are erasing specific traumatic memories, we use mental distractions so that you are not dwelling on the trauma.

The healing mechanism works quietly in the background as we have conversations about the best things in your life and your happy memories.

Through these stories I also learn of the gifts you have to offer the world.

Sometimes clients find it difficult to remember good things in life so we use neutral distractions or metaphorical images that help with the healing. There are endless possibilities. Often we end up laughing together.

My work is deeply intuitive. I have learned to trust my instinct and to know when to gently intervene or steer the practice. I'm feeling with you and sensing what needs to be done.

This is what my clients have written about me:

'Calm, gentle, sensitive, compassionate, totally present, intuitive, creative, very safe, empathetic, nurturing, friendly and human, a delicate presence and warmth, respectful.'

One of my clients said, *'Robin approaches every session with such creativity, openness, hope, and trust in an individual's ability to heal and in the incredible power of Havening.'*

These philosophies of practice also shape how I see the world and create real possibilities for healing the damage done to our communities and the natural environment. It makes me hopeful in these times of trouble.

8. A BETTER WORLD STARTS WITH ME

While this book has focused on addressing and healing our own personal lives, I believe we have a much bigger commitment to make – to building a better world, for our children and our communities. We each can be powerful in that role but only when we let go of our own wounds.

Our personal trauma, and the trauma of the wider world turns out to be closely related. Indeed, some say that a rational response to the modern world is to be acutely anxious and depressed. But as we witness the miracle of our own rapid healing, we realise that the wider world could also transform.

When we let go of trying to fix the world and instead focus on healing ourselves, healing our communities and the natural world, we see amazing results.

The clients I especially want to help are those who are ready to *commit* to healing their own wounds and being the people who inspire positive change around them. When you are living as the best version of yourself, the possibilities are endless.

How we can heal our world

I believe we are at a turning point in history. I'm writing this book in the midst of the Coronavirus pandemic, which has brutally exposed the divisions in our society and the corruption of our economic and political systems. It's the socially, economically and racially disadvantaged who are bearing the brunt of the pandemic.

Also, Coronavirus has temporarily displaced from our attention the climate crisis and environmental collapse, which are accelerating at a terrifying rate.

At the same time we see horrifying rates of anxiety, depression, self-harm, suicide and violence in our communities. Adults are burdened with chronic disease caused by unhealthy lifestyles. For the first time in over a century, we are actually seeing a fall in life expectancy in wealthy countries, such as the UK.

All these crises have the same ultimate cause.

Fundamentally, we are all deeply immersed in a cultural myth of separation and dominance, which is driving us to ruin.

The reality is that we are profoundly connected to each other and to the natural world. When we tap into the power of that connection, we witness miracles of self-healing. But when our whole society is built on a myth of separation, we are heading for disaster.

In our modern society, we act as if we are separate beings competing for attention and riches, and that humankind is separate from nature. In our culture, humankind's role is to dominate and control nature for the extraction of wealth – not to live in harmony with nature.

Thus we profit from natural resources without regard for the long-term effects of pollution, degradation and ruin. We act as if our own health and wellbeing is not in any way connected to the living world. Decades after scientists conclusively established the reality of climate change, we continue to plunder the Earth and drive us ever-faster towards environmental collapse.

We regard forests as a source of timber, not the lungs of the world. Soil becomes just a substrate for growing crops, not a complex living system. Animals are separated from their natural environment and farmed in factories, pumped full of antibiotics and drugs. We poison the land and rivers with agricultural chemicals.

Not so long ago, many of our human needs were met in community, in systems of mutual care and support. But now our childcare, eldercare, food production, education, and material needs have been out-sourced to an economic system owned and controlled by people who are not part of our community.

If we don't have enough money, we are forced to go without many of our basic needs. Our competitive economic system creates grotesque inequality, with growing rates of poverty and disadvantage, and all of the social and physical ills that accompany this.

As our communities break down, authorities respond with increasing police violence, surveillance and ever-more draconian laws. Vast numbers of people are locked up in prison, mostly those from the non-white community, the dispossessed, the disadvantaged, and those with traumatic upbringings.

Our politics have become ever more partisan and intolerant – continually demonizing the 'opposition'. We have lost empathy, compassion and kindness. There is little room for partnership or collaboration in creating laws that address our growing crises.

The forces of individualism and separation are tearing apart our lives and our communities. The answer is healing and connection. Powerful change is possible much more quickly than you think.

The myth of separation is deeply pervasive, even shaping our science and knowledge. We have adopted a materialistic form of science, which sees the Universe and Nature as dead and meaningless, nothing more than a collection of atomic particles.

Our economic systems reinforce this idea that every natural resource is just a commodity to be owned, controlled and sold for a price. Even our ideas, stories and songs become intellectual property.

These materialistic systems of thinking and economics pervade all of our world, our science and education, our healthcare, our corporations and public sectors.

Even human consciousness is perceived as merely the result of chemical reactions in the brain, not part of anything greater than ourselves. Modern medical science has reduced the human being into a set of molecules and structures.

The idea that illness is in any way 'meaningful' or that humans have self-healing capacity is systematically removed from Western medical science.

Why else would the medical response to complex lifestyle problems such as anxiety, depression, stress, obesity, diabetes, or hypertension be limited to a ten-minute doctor appointment followed by a drug prescription?

If we think for a moment about the word 'disease', we can see that the origin of the word is 'dis-ease'. In other words, many physical illnesses have their origins in our chronic stress and emotional problems. If you erase the trauma, you can cure many physical health problems, including cases of chronic pain.

It's hardly surprising that so many people seek complementary or alternative healthcare, where the practitioners bring a holistic approach to treating the whole person. Even if doctors angrily denounce such treatments as not 'evidence-based', many patients do well through the therapeutic connection with their practitioner, which stimulates their own self-healing mechanisms.

Our healthcare system is not actually a health system, instead we submit to a 'medicated sickness' system of chronic disease. Of course, this is massively profitable for pharmaceutical and healthcare corporations, who have turned illness into a commodity and patients into revenue systems.

You begin to see how powerfully our myth of separation shapes our science and the way we think about and organize many different sections of society.

Our education systems are not designed to create great citizens and to equip them with real-life skills; rather they are systems to condition children and young adults to submit to economic and corporate systems. They teach individualism and competition, rather than collaboration and sharing.

Our academic institutions are now turning into corporations, where knowledge is to be protected and sold for a price, and profit seems to be more important than learning.

Our penal systems are designed to punish and control, not to rehabilitate inmates to be good citizens. It's hardly surprising that 70% to 80% of inmates commit new crimes after release from prison.

These ways of thinking are destroying the planet and making us all sick. And it is just a cultural myth, with little relationship to reality.

A connected world

In truth, we are all deeply connected, to each other and to the natural world. The real world is a much more magical and marvelous place than the version of reality we wrap ourselves in.

All indigenous cultures are deeply integrated with nature and they incorporate spiritual beliefs that connect each individual person to a much broader reality. Ancient wisdom texts, such as the 'Tao Te Ching', also emphasise profound interconnection and reciprocity.

Every action we take on the world impacts us in return: every act of generosity and caring ultimately benefits us and every act of violence and destruction harms us.

Human beings are deeply connected, not just through our speech, and body language but also energetically. We all experience this connection in every day life: some people give us positive energy, some drain us; some agitate us and some help us feel calm and safe. All of us are affected by the global agitation and fear surrounding Coronavirus.

Then we add the dimension of touch. Human touch is absolutely essential to our wellbeing. We are social creatures. Our sense of safety, soothing, connection and love are critically dependent on touch.

As I mentioned in the earlier chapter on the science of Havening, neuroscientists just recently discovered a whole class of nerves in our skin, which exist only to detect and transmit the sensation of soothing touch. Signals from these nerves are wired into our emotional centres and radically change our brain state. Being in receipt of soothing touch causes the release of hormones like oxytocin – the hormone of bonding and love.

Loving touch is so crucial to our development that children who are deprived of touch can't grow their brains properly. You might recall the awful stories of small children abandoned in Romanian orphanages in the 1980's and 90's. Deprived of human affection and contact, the structure and function of their developing brains were permanently damaged.

The Earth is a living being

The planet Earth is a living being, of profound interconnection and complexity, every part essential for the survival of the whole.

As humans we forget that the very atmosphere we breathe is created and maintained by plants. In every breath we take, the life-giving oxygen is that made by plants. We breathe out high concentrations of carbon dioxide. Why doesn't our breath cause runaway global warming? Because living plants absorb carbon dioxide.

The forests are literally the lungs of our living world – they absorb carbon dioxide and emit oxygen to keep humans and all creatures alive. Forests and wetlands also regulate the water cycle – they absorb, store and release water as liquid and vapour.

Rainforests don't just exist in places with high rainfall – they actually create their own climate and rain. Globally, about 40% of all rainfall derives from water vapour transpired by forests; in the Amazon, it is 70%. Take away the trees and you eventually end up with desert.

The extremes of climate we are witnessing are not so much the result of gradual global warming, as the widespread destruction of the organs of the planet that *regulate* our climate. Our world is tipping into multiple organ failure and will soon need intensive care.

Our responses to the climate crisis are still stuck in the thinking that arises from the myth of separation. Wouldn't it be better to ask how we can heal the planet, rather than endlessly pursue technical solutions for carbon reduction?

The miracles of human healing I share in this book serve as a illustration for much wider possibilities. As I was learning

Havening Techniques, I also began to observe the most inspiring examples of rapid healing in our natural environment.

The small town where I live, Raglan in New Zealand, is set on a beautiful harbour. Twenty years ago the harbour was practically dead.

All the native forests on the surrounding land have disappeared, to be replaced with grazing land. The cattle and sheep erode the bare hills and trample the stream beds. As a result, vast amounts of silt ran into the harbour, accompanied by faecal material and agricultural chemicals. The fish disappeared from the harbor and the sandy beaches were covered ankle-deep in mud.

An intrepid band of community volunteers decided to address the problem. Their solution was simple: fence off a narrow strip of land on either side of the waterways in the farmland, and plant native trees and bushes in the riparian margin. They grew the plants from seeds collected in the vestiges of the native forest.

The environmental engineers were not impressed – they said it would take at least fifty years to make any appreciable impact on water quality. They were wrong.

Today the harbor is utterly transformed. The beaches are clean and the fish are fast multiplying in the harbor. We have regular visits from orca, swimming past the beaches and the wharf.

In the seven years we have lived in Raglan the pace of change is astonishing. The tidal flats are now stabilized and covered in dense mats of sea grass where there was none just a few years ago.

The formerly bare beaches are now littered with shells because the shellfish are flourishing in the harbor once again, together with the wading birds. Nature has taken over the job of cleaning the harbour. All it needed was a helping hand.

Similarly dramatic results are seen in trials of regenerative agriculture. For forty years, the Rodale Institute in the USA (https://rodaleinstitute.org) has been conducting side-by-side comparison of conventional and organic agriculture. After five years of organic practice, the soil health is restored and crop yields are higher than conventional agriculture.

Crops are more drought resistant and contain higher levels of protein and nutrients. Energy consumption is reduced 45%, carbon emissions are reduced 40%, and farmer profits are three to six times higher. No toxic chemicals are leached into the waterways

Large-scale change is possible in a short time scale. The entire state of Sikkim in India banned agricultural chemicals and turned to multi-crop organic agriculture. The yields of crops fell initially but were restored within three years. After five years the crop yields exceeded that produced by intensive, chemical driven monoculture.

This style of agriculture is much more labour intensive – but isn't that a good thing, creating healthy and meaningful jobs when unemployment is soaring? Input costs are less and profits are higher.

The formerly depleted soil is now rich with organic matter, bacteria and fungi that support healthy and vigorous plants. The soil now stores so much carbon, it's estimated that if we turned all of world agriculture to regenerative practices, and moved to a largely plant-based diet, we'd dramatically slow global warming.

The entire eco-system rapidly recovers, the rivers run clean, the insects, birds and fish return. Indeed Sikkim has a boom in tourism because it has become a natural paradise.

A new cultural story of connection and inter-being offers us solutions to our most complex problems - a world brimming with capacity for self-healing and regeneration, a world of abundance and meaningful connection.

The healing practice I offer is a window into this magical world. It's a practice based on intimate human connection, which activates a remarkable capacity for self-healing.

I witness in my clients a powerful, intuitive, healing wisdom, that shapes their healing journey, always keeping them safe. I believe that all living systems have this capacity.

This healing seems miraculous from the perspective of the myth of separation – or from the medical science I was trained in. But what if this is the ordinary potential of a connected world? I think the new science of self-healing is the beginning of a revolution in how we perceive the world.

To flourish, we need to live in community, to have a sense of identity and belonging. We need to give and experience kindness, generosity, joy, and laughter. We need to show empathy and compassion to those less fortunate, to look after our vulnerable.

None of those things can be replaced with an online world, despite the hype of the big tech companies. If the Coronavirus pandemic and social-distancing has taught me one thing, it's how sacred is human touch and connection.

It's time to reconnect, to connect to each other as human beings. Not on computer screens and mobile phones but face

to face. We need compassion and kindness, caring and generosity.

We need to start moving more and more of our life away from the monetary economy so that we barter, exchange, lend, help each other, recycle and repair – all within the setting of communities of mutual support. We need to reconnect the generations, not separate them into childcare and eldercare facilities, all of which cost us money.

We need to eat real food, grown in our local communities – not manufactured products that come out of a factory. We need to invest in regenerative agriculture and to stop poisoning the land, the rivers and the wildlife. When we look after the land, nature returns a magnificent bounty.

To create a connected world, we first need to connect to ourselves

It's time to choose. The change starts with us. We must attend to our own healing first. Through that healing, we learn the power of connection, and the self-healing and self-regenerating capacity of people and of nature.

The Universe is generous. When we reconnect we find more joyfulness, healing and blessing. I want to live in that world. Will you join me?

9. FINDING HELP

There are only so many clients I can personally treat in a lifetime. I really want the benefits of Havening to spread far and wide. The healing method not only promises a revolution in mental health, and the treatment of addiction, it also has a potentially huge impact on our physical health as well.

I hope you have found this book helpful, whatever your life situation and wherever you are in the world. So many of my clients blame themselves for their problems and I hope now you have a better understanding of why you struggle in the way you do, and how it's possible to leave your past behind. Imagine how it would feel to experience life as your best and most authentic self!

The healing techniques I describe are available in many places and there are hundreds of practitioners who can work with you in person, or online.

Make sure that the professional you work with is a Certified Havening Practitioner, who therefore has been properly trained, coached and certified in the application of these powerful techniques.

Our first duty as practitioners is to keep clients safe. Some clients with complex trauma can be very vulnerable. These practices should not be used in untrained hands.

You can search for a Havening Techniques practitioner on the Havening website using https://havening.org/directory/grid/practitioners-list-grid and entering your location. Full profiles and contact details of all Certified Havening Practitioners are listed on the pages. The website also has further information about Havening, including details of where you can access training.

Internationally, the Havening community is very close-knit. We share a secure online space where the best practitioners in the world support each other, offer practice groups and training sessions, and help out with challenging cases.

The majority of Havening Practitioners are experienced therapists who have added Havening to their existing knowledge of NLP, EMDR, hypnotherapy, counselling, psychotherapy, medicine, nursing, midwifery and other professional skills. Many say that Havening is the most powerful technique they have ever used.

If you can't find a Havening Practitioner close to you, then online care is an option. Although it's not my personal preference, there are many Havening Practitioners who are skilled at providing care online and have found strategies to overcome the limitations I mention.

In New Zealand

If you live in New Zealand, you can access my help directly. I practice in the Waikato region. The nearest city, Hamilton, is about 40 minutes drive from the small town of Raglan where I have my home and clinic.

I want you to think carefully about how you get the best value. Many of us have accessed some form of counselling, therapy or coaching on a sessional basis. Havening can support and complement the work you have already done.

But sometimes we just need to press the reset button and commit to making a major life change. With intermittent therapy sessions it's too easy to fall back into the same old patterns and struggles.

A healing retreat has the power to change your life trajectory. Imagine how powerful the impact could be, working one-on-one over a period of days, releasing your trauma, finding your strengths, clarifying your values, building your confidence, discovering your self-worth, transforming your relationships, and building a new identity.

Imagine becoming truly resilient and having a secure and calm foundation to deal with life's challenges.

Most of all, how great would it be to offer your gifts and talents to the world?

Don't just do it for you. Do it for all your friends, family and loved ones. When you change, the whole world changes around you.

I see huge positive ripple effects spreading far and wide all around my clients. The ones who are most successful are those who commit to turning their lives around, who decide to make this investment in their future.

What I offer

See my Neuroscience of Healing website (neuroscienceofhealing.org) for the full range of services, including training in Havening Techniques. I run the Raglan Academy of Havening and my trainees provide low-cost care to our community, while practising under my supervision.

The span of my care includes:
- A single session (online or in person) to erase a traumatic memory and free you from that burden
- One or more sessions to cure a phobia
- A course of in-person sessions to deal with more complex trauma
- Residential healing retreats for intensive,

one-on-one healing and coaching to turn your life around

Healing retreats
The work I love the most, is helping clients completely turn their life around. My wife Meredith and I offer five-day retreats in our home. I offer Havening and life coaching. Meredith is an energy healer (*BARS / Access Consciousness*) and an *'Enhances Awareness Program' (EAP)* Mentor. We offer:

- An in-depth assessment of your needs and desires
- Baseline scoring of your mental wellbeing
- Consecutive days of trauma healing and coaching
- Energy healing
- Guided walks connecting to nature
- Enhancing your awareness
- Clarifying your values
- Learning your character strengths and gifts
- Creating a secure foundation of self-worth and confidence
- Building a new identity
- Follow-up sessions as you build a new life

To this we add comfortable private accommodation, which is peaceful, welcoming and self-contained. We have amazing views over the harbour and ocean, and enjoy wonderful sunsets. We'll provide nourishing home-cooked food including produce from our garden. Part of the healing process is connection to nature and we provide guided walks in the beautiful native forest and on the beach. You can decide your own needs for nurturing company or private time alone.

The Raglan town centre, harbour, and beaches are just a few minutes' walk from our home. Raglan has many wonderful shops, restaurants and galleries.

We ask you to commit this time to yourself, in a retreat fully away from work and family. This is *your* time to build the foundations of a new life. Your loved ones will thank you for it!

See full details on my website: neuroscienceofhealing.org

MORE RESOURCES

There are two other excellent books about Havening Techniques. The first is, *'Fifteen Minutes to Freedom: The Power and Promise of Havening Techniques'* by Harry Pickens, who is an amazing Havening Practitioner and Trainer in the USA. Harry interviews the developers of Havening and many of the practioners, gathering stories of the amazing impact of Havening on peoples' live.

The second book is, *'When the Past is Always Present'* by Ronald Ruden MD, where he lays out his many years of research and scientific insights into the nature of trauma and the development of Havening Techniques.

You can purchase these books from Amazon or any other major bookseller.

I have a collection of self-Havening videos on my YouTube channel (https://www.youtube.com/user/DrRobinYoungson) which have proved very popular:

- A 60-second 'anxiety hack'
- A ten-minute, daily, self-healing practice
- A thirty-minute, in-depth experience of self-Havening and how you can reshape your neurology
- Self-Havening for a sudden, debilitating injury
- Self-Havening to remain well in pregnancy

You can purchase copies of all my books from the shop on my website, or from Amazon and other major online booksellers.

You can watch my TEDx Talk, *'Perfectly broken and ready to heal'* at https://youtu.be/jTYSzLtbYTU

DID YOU LOVE MY BOOK?

P lease visit Amazon and post a brief review on my book at amazon.com/dp/B08K7BN6GZ/

ABOUT THE AUTHOR

Robin Youngson

Dr Robin Youngson, MA MB ChB FANZCA, is a Certified Havening Practitioner and Trainer, and is a recently retired Anaesthetic Specialist with a long career in the public health service in the UK and New Zealand.

As an international campaigner, speaker and author, Robin has been a leading voice calling for humane and compassionate healthcare. Together with his wife Meredith, Robin was the founder of Hearts in Healthcare, an international social movement. Robin and Meredith have brought their work to fifteen countries and Robin's book, 'TIME TO CARE – How to love your patients and your job' is translated into Dutch, German and Hungarian.

In parallel with his clinical career, Robin has also been an outstanding health leader, and pioneer in patient safety and quality improvement. He has been an advisor to the New Zealand Government and the World Health Organisation.

In 2016, the New Zealand Medical Association gave Robin their highest prize, the Chair's Award, for outstanding contribution to the health of New Zealand, especially in recognition of his pioneering work on compassionate healthcare.

You can learn about Robin's deep reflections on compassionate leadership through his TEDx talk and also his book, 'From HERO to HEALER – Awakening the Inner Activist'.

Robin and Meredith have three grown-up daughters and two grandchildren. They live happily in the small, seaside town of Raglan in the North Island of NZ. Robin is an avid landscaper, builder and restorer.

He delights in reviving old furniture and tools, recycling materials, and building things that will last a lifetime. His therapy room is a testament to his creativity and his ability to see the potential in both people and things.

Having started his career as an engineer, before studying medicine, Robin can turn his hand to many trades. He offers his skills by contributing to the Raglan Time Bank, offering free repairs and help especially to those who live alone. He also loves walking in the native forest and going for long cycle rides in the country around Raglan.

PRAISE FOR AUTHOR

From HERO to HEALER - "powerful, insightful and life-affirming. A recipe to empower each of us to be change makers not only of ourselves but of the world."

- JAMES R DOTY MD, BESTSELLING AUTHOR OF 'INTO THE MAGIC SHOP'

TIME TO CARE - "If you read only one book about healthcare in our lifetime, whether you are a patient or a professional, let this be the book"

- MICHAEL BROPHY, IRISH SOCIETY FOR QUALITY AND SAFETY IN HEALTHCARE

TIME TO CARE - "Well researched, beautifully written and deeply inspiring this is one book I would recommend all clinicians to read at the beginning of their careers and constantly revisit many times throughout."

- PROFESSOR PAUL GILBERT, DIRECTOR OF THE COMPASSIONATE MIND FOUNDATION

TIME TO CARE - "At the critical interface between patients and health professionals TIME TO CARE offers some extremely constructive ways of salvaging care in current frenetic health service environments."

- PROFESSOR JENNY CARRYER, EXEC DIRECTOR NEW ZEALAND COLLEGE OF NURSES

TIME TO CARE - "Youngson speaks with great wisdom and authority as a highly trained clinician and senior health leader who has extensively researched the literature on compassion, leadership and positive psychology; however, it is his experience as a compassionate human being that shines through the pages of this book."

- MARC COHEN, PROFESSOR OF COMPLEMENTARY MEDICINE RMIT UNIVERSITY

"TIME TO CARE offers many practical ways to embody change and a real sense of hope for a brighters future. TIME TO CARE shows us where the light switch is - all we have to do is act."

- JOHN KEASLEY, PROFESSOR OF MEDICINE (CON-JOINT) AT UNIVERSITY OF NSW AND UNIVERSITY OF WILLONGONG

From HERO to HEALER - "Brillian, poignant, important... fundamental to building the next generation of leaders."

- MAUREEN BISOGNANO, PRESIDENT EMERITA AND SENIOR FELLOW, INSTITUTE OF HEALTHCARE IMPROVEMENT

From HERO to HEALER - "This book is a gift to us. Robin shows us how to confront our own wisdom and ways of doing things, to consider and embrace a new path of possibilities. Truly the book is a winner."

- MARILYN TURKOVICH, DIRECTOR CHARTER FOR COMPASSION

From HERO to HEALER - "The very heart of UPLIFT spirit, beautifully expressed in your wonderful book. Already sharing it all over with great joy."

- BHARAT MITRA, FOUNDER OF UPLIFT

BOOKS BY THIS AUTHOR

Time To Care - How To Love Your Patients And Your Job

In today's beleaguered healthcare system, burdened with epidemic levels of stress, depression and burn-out, TIME to CARE offers health professionals the opportunity of renewal. Here are the secrets to building a happy and fulfilling practice, wellbeing and resilience. Youngson bravely relates his own transition, from a detached clinician to a champion for humane whole-patient care; at times poignant, sometimes funny but always brutally honest. TIME to CARE offers a deeply compassionate and insightful account of a health system that is failing both patients and practitioners all over the world. But there's more.... Drawing on advances in neuroscience and positive psychology, and tapping the power of appreciative inquiry, Youngson conveys in clear and simple language how health workers can strengthen their hearts, learn the skills of compassionate caring, and rise above institutional limitations to transform patient care.... and rediscover their vocation. Already translated into three languages, TIME to CARE is recommended reading for today's health professionals, students, health leaders, patients, and all those passionate about re-humanizing healthcare.

From Hero To Healer: Awakening The Inner Activist

If you are a social or environmental activist, reading this little book might be the best investment you ever make. If I had known and understood these lessons earlier, it might have spared me a decade of wasted effort.

I'm a practising doctor in New Zealand and an internationally renowned leader in compassionate healthcare. I really care about building a better world. Here's the question that really bugs me: "Despite our persistent efforts, and high-profile campaigns involving millions of people, why are we not making more progress on social and environmental issues? We are witnessing more poverty, more inequality, more chronic disease, more social breakdown, worsening pollution, and ever-increasing carbon emissions?"

Could it be that the strategies we employ as activists are actually sustaining the problems we're trying to address?

As honestly as I can, I share with you the five BIGGEST mistakes I made in a decade of campaigning, and how my counter-intuitive new strategies led to international success.

My book builds on a TEDx talk I gave in 2016, entitled "Perfectly broken and ready to heal". I really hope this book helps you and your great work.

Printed in Great Britain
by Amazon